In 1943, invisibility experiments were conducted *aboard the "USS Eldridge" that resulted in full scale teleportation of the ship and crew. Popularly known as the "Philadelphia Experiment", these events resulted in paranormal experiences and mental disablement for the majority of the sailors involved.*

After World War II, a massive research project *was undertaken t   ⸱⸱⸱ bottom of the Philadelphia Experiment and   ⸱⸱⸱ᵗⁱonal secrets of the Unified Fiel   ᵤl devel-opments event   aircraft. Additionally, a   ᵢcted that was far more bizarre. Whᵢⱼ ⸱   stand how human beings could survive in other aᵤₙ.. .ons, people were subjected to experiments whereby their minds were interfaced with radio waves and vacuum tube computers. Psychic abilities were monitored and eventually har-nessed until time itself could be manipulated. The most extravagant of these experiments took place at the Montauk Air Force Station at Montauk Point, New York and have been popularized in the first book of this series, "The Montauk Project: Experiments in Time".*

Montauk Revisited: Adventures in Synchronicity *digs deeper into the mysteries of Montauk and offers countless stories and corroborations that show the project did actually exist. In a new twist to the story, powerful occult factors are discovered to lurk behind the entire scenario of the Montauk Project. An amazing search is undertaken which takes us far beyond the scope of the first book. The secrets uncovered eventually lead us to the very core of creation itself.*

■ **The stars await.**

*C*over art:

represents the invocation of Babalon,
the mother of the universe, which equates to
understanding. *The Montauk Project* symbolizes
the dark forces and decadence of the patriarchal
power system that has ruled during the Age of Pisces.
Babalon comes to our rescue as the feminine
principle which will balance the tragedies
of the past and usher us into Aquarius,
the Age of Enlightenment and trust.

MONTAUK REVISITED

ADVENTURES IN SYNCHRONICITY

PRESTON B. NICHOLS
& PETER MOON

ILLUSTRATED BY NINA HELMS

SkyBooks

NEW YORK

Montauk Revisited: Adventures in Synchronicity
Copyright © 1994 by Preston B. Nichols and Peter Moon
First printing, January 1994

Cover art and illustrations by Nina Helms
Typography and book design by Creative Circle Inc.
Editorial Consultants, Margo Geiger, Lin Giliberti
Published by: Sky Books
     Box 769
     Westbury, New York 11590

Library of Congress Cataloging-in-Publication Data

Nichols, Preston B. / Moon, Peter
   Montauk Revisited: Adventures in Synchronicity
by Preston B. Nichols and Peter Moon
   240 pages, illustrated
   ISBN 0-9631889-1-7
1. Occult 2. Time travel 3. Anomalies
Library of Congress Catalog Card Number 93-084992

This book is dedicated to the memory of
Jan Brice, a fellow seeker on the path, and the man
who photographed "The Beast".

*There is a mystery
that underlies all other mysteries
and we call that the Tao.*

—*old Chinese proverb*

CONTENTS

MONTAUK POINT ■

MONTAUK ■

SOUTHAMPTON
■

BROOKHAVEN
■

■ FIRE ISLAND

WESTBURY
■

■ QUEENS

■
MANHATTAN

■
BROOKLYN

LONG ISLAND

PRELUDE

A moderately clear day in Los Angeles will reveal a range of mountains to the north. Interestingly, if you ask the average local the name of these mountains, they will usually draw a blank stare and tell you they don't know. This manifested ignorance concerning an everyday sight is indicative of an even greater ignorance concerning a mysterious sequence of events that began in these mountains in the 1930's.

The name of this range is the San Gabriel Mountains and is readily available to anyone who cares to look on a map. Rising above the other peaks is Mount Wilson, home of the Wilson Observatory. To the west of Mount Wilson and just behind the Devil's Gate Dam in Pasadena is Arroyo Seco, the canyon from which the now famous Jet Propulsion Laboratory was sprung. Our mystery begins with the genesis of JPL and the rocket scientist who brought the space age into being: John Whiteside "Jack" Parsons.

Parsons had studied information at Cal Tech concerning the idea of a rocket powered airplane. Although he had no formal education, he was a self-trained chemist and had already been experimenting with small rockets. Parsons approached Cal Tech about his own ideas and his brilliance was recognized by the authorities there. Accordingly, an entire unit was set up to conduct further rocket research.

The Army Air Corps took immediate interest in this activity which ultimately led to a contract with Jack Parsons and his partners. They formed Aerojet General Corporation and worked under that auspices. (This company is still around today as an active defense contractor.) The first task for Parsons and company was to develop rocket propulsion to assist in the take off of heavily laden aircraft. Although this work concerned rockets, the name "jet" was used; hence, the name "Jet Propulsion Laboratory".

Although Parsons was not the only one who made the space age possible, his contribution was considered so pivotal that a crater on the moon was named after him to honor his genius. But Jack Parsons was far more than a brilliant rocket scientist. He was not only a colorful and popular personality but also an occultist and practicing magician. In fact, his sphere of influence was so great that rumors consistently circulated (and are still heard even today) that the other scientists worshipped him and practiced strange rites under his direction.

All of this no doubt disturbed the Government authorities who monitored early rocketry. Parsons' brilliance, independent philosophy and popularity amongst the other scientists was perceived as a potential threat to the Government status quo. Consequently, a Naval intelligence officer was sent in to Parsons' group. As is so typical with bumbling Government authorities, the Navy's plan backfired. The Naval officer had his own agenda. In fact, he was just as brilliant as Parsons, only in a different area: human psychology.

This Naval officer had studied the most avant-garde and top secret psychiatric records in the United States. All sorts of wild experimentation had gone on during the war and he was privy to it. Much of this research had to do with narcosynthesis. People were questioned under "truth serum" and countless areas of abnormal psychology were explored. Some of these included mental and emotional blocks as well as the paranormal. These studies, in part, opened the door to the consciousness of aliens and their influence upon mankind.

The name of this Naval officer was none other than L. Ron Hubbard who would engage Parsons as a friend and participate in his magical workings. Their activities and work together are still shrouded in mystery today.

At first glance, it might seem that the genesis of American rocketry could not have much to do with the Montauk Project. However, recent events have revealed a mysterious occult connection between Montauk and the early days of the Jet Propulsion Laboratory. This mystery runs very deep and will be explored later in this book, but the first thing to know is that *The Montauk Project* would never have been written had it not been for the liaison of Jack Parsons and L. Ron Hubbard.

Parsons was assassinated in 1952 by an explosion in his laboratory. I was born down the road six months later (this is not meant to imply that I was Jack Parsons) and my life followed a rather incredible path that eventually lead me to the doors of L. Ron Hubbard, Preston Nichols and Jack Parsons' wife, Marjorie Cameron (an artist, poet, revolutionary and an extremely feared occultist in her own right). For the most part, my meetings and involvements with these people were not consciously planned. They seemed guided by a higher power that was part of some overall scheme.

My first encounter with these remarkable people was with Hubbard. My relationship with him was not that of a routine Scientologist as I was trusted with a lot of intimate information. I also helped to handle his personal affairs. More importantly, I would learn from him the various factors behind implantation and manipulation of the human race. If it were not for this rather thorough education process, I do not believe I would have been able to approach Preston Nichols or deal with the various psychological oddities that one encounters in researching the Montauk Project.

This is the legacy that I emerged from in order to write *The Montauk Project: Experiments in Time* with Preston. Had I not been clued in on the above information, it is quite likely that the first book would never have come to pass.

It is as if Hubbard passed a torch to me that would shine light on Montauk and then lead me back full circle to a strange encounter with the wife of his magician friend, Jack Parsons. That story will be told later on. For now, just realize that the events that preceded my involvement in all this came as a direct result of three very famous and powerful magicians.

This is where our mystery begins.

I

INTRODUCTION

Writing *The Montauk Project* was a most intriguing personal experience. There were more bizarre occurrences than I could hope to put on paper. Certainly among the most interesting have been those of working with Preston Nichols and Duncan Cameron. As I am frequently asked questions about the nature of these two people, I will start by giving a quick overview on who they actually are.

Preston is a walking talking security risk as far as the intelligence community is concerned. There is no question in my own mind that he has been involved with secret government and intelligence projects. It is also obvious to anyone who knows him well that he has been schooled in information that is beyond the boundaries of higher learning. Preston remembers studying textbooks and information that is privy only to those in secret sectors of the military industrial complex. Though his only degree is a Bachelor's in engineering, he estimates that he has obtained the equivalent of Ph.D.'s in physics, psychology, theology and engineering. His opinions are most definitely sought after by prominent people in the scientific community.

On the more personal side, there is a good sense of humor and a strong psychic streak in him which he plays down, even to himself. Preston is by nature a friendly person but experience has taught him to be extremely careful of whom he trusts.

For whatever reason, his experiences and life seem to foster constant intrigue. Sometimes I feel that he may be stirring much of it up himself. Other times it is clear that there is a deeper thread at work and there is a much bigger scenario of which he is just a part. Preston's life is loaded with mystery, and I have only been exposed to a part of it. Although it is a delicate area for him, it is my hope that he will cooperate and do an autobiography in the near future.

If you think that Preston is a mystery to figure out, then go and try Duncan Cameron. He is one of the most curious human enigmas that I have ever been exposed to. Duncan is a very private individual yet can be extremely charismatic and sociable at times. While Preston speaks with scientific terms and references that are quite detailed yet out of the range of college text books, Duncan does the same with metaphysics. He speaks quite eloquently at times with access to an enormous amount of information that apparently comes from some mysterious source. Duncan says he has an I.Q. of about 100. This is hard to believe when you hear him speak. I think he would score poorly on such a test because while he is absolutely brilliant in some areas, in others he is untrained or simply not interested. It is my hope that Duncan will also do a book someday. Currently, he is a carpenter by profession and works with Preston on almost a daily basis probing various psychic phenomena. He very badly wants to clean up the bad effects from the Montauk Project and has said that he would like to someday sponsor a foundation that would help care for some of the victims.

I also believe that both Preston and Duncan have been subject to programming by the intelligence community. This is most obvious in Duncan but it would apply to anyone who had involvement with the Montauk Project. Preston has apparently broken the majority of the programming although there are some people who would disagree.

Have they travelled in time?

I'm not exactly sure but if I had to place a bet with an impartial judge, I'd say yes. If time is an illusion and all possibilities are happening in some universe, time travel can be taken for granted. It is my personal belief that we are moving into an era where the consciousness of time is reverting to what it was many aeons ago. Duncan and Preston are simply pioneering the areas that most of us have left unexplored.

It is not fair to mention these two without mentioning Duncan's half brother, Al Bielek. He is not only a scientist and a metaphysician, but remembers being aboard the *U.S.S. Eldridge* during the Philadelphia Experiment. If his experiences are not to be believed, his contacts in the intelligence community are noteworthy to say the least. Al is perhaps more dedicated to resolving the conspiracies behind the secret government than anyone I've met.

I don't claim to have secret government contacts or to be a time traveller like Al or Duncan, but I have studied and dealt with implants for over twenty years. Implantation has everything to do with the nature of knowing exactly who you are and who might have caused you to think in ways that are not in your own interest. It is a vast subject and is right at the heart of the cosmic conspiracy. There have been many articles and shows about abductions and implantation, but most of the practitioners I've seen on television know very little of the entire scope. However, their efforts do seem to help the general public come to a better understanding of the subject.

Needless to say, implantation and making people

forget is what the Montauk Project was all about. Had I not had extensive experience in this area, I do not believe that I would have been able to get close to Preston and write his story. As a matter of fact, after the book was out and doing well, he told me later that other writers had attempted to work with him. They would become frightened and depart as soon as they began to get an idea that his stories were indeed real.

When I first heard the Montauk story from Preston, I was intrigued because it had all the earmarks of being a real live implant station. I'd witnessed their effects and had dealt with them but had never met anyone who actually worked at one or knew the various technologies, with the exception of Hubbard. Preston had new information for me about how people are programmed and his insights are vast. Duncan and Al were both with Preston when I heard the initial story and they greatly contributed to my understanding. As I left them and rode home in an astonished state of mind, a thought suddenly ran through my mind: "So this is why I came to Long Island". This was not a thought from my ordinary thought processes. I would later look back and realize that I had moved to Long Island a few weeks before the Montauk Project culminated on August 12, 1983. The strings of synchronicity were already at work in my personal life. Thus, you have a quick overview of how it became my destiny to become the scribe for the Montauk investigation.

In this book, we will attempt to satisfy some of the curiosity concerning *The Montauk Project* and also give a sane perspective on what this story is about, its relative truth and what are the implications of it all.

We will begin with a brief discussion of legends and how they apply to the truth. Next, I will give a chronicle of my actual experiences in writing about Montauk. This will not only give a different view on the whole affair but will corroborate some of Preston's stories. Next, Preston will give an update on startling events that have occurred since *The Montauk Project* was published. I will then follow this up with yet further information that has come to us. The plot thickens...

PART
I

BY PETER MOON

1

LEGEND AND MYTHOLOGY

Perhaps the most important point in dealing with the phenomena of Montauk is to realize that we are dealing with "the stuff of which dreams are made". We are directly tapping into the creative zone of consciousness. The creative process in humans is not only our closest approach to the Creator, it is the function which has given rise to myths and legends throughout the ages. When we are dealing with this subject, it is important to delineate exactly what is a legend and what is its relationship to the truth. Joseph Campbell has made extremely lucid comments about this relationship in his various talks and writings on the subject of myths. I am going to offer a simplified view from my perspective.

Legends abound in all primitive people. They also occur in popular culture, giving rise to folk heroes and the like. A legend arises when there is something noteworthy to describe. What is considered noteworthy is determined by the people involved. It would presumably be in direct relationship to the survival value or thought value of the concept being described. It could also have humor value.

For example, if a tribe of people were invaded and fought off their enemies through the bravery of a great warrior, stories and admiration would be due the warrior. In time, a legend would arise depicting the warrior with various attributes. In times of battle, the witchdoctor might even invoke the spirit of the dead warrior. Without consideration for any spiritual activity that may be at work, the tribe would at least be concentrating and focusing on the archetype of such a warrior and would rally around the symbol in order to invigorate their fighting ability.

This is a very simple example. Legends would also arise about lovers, mothers, crops and all the various gods which one can read about in mythology books. It can get very complex. The main point is that the legend survives because it is describing something that has inherent survival or thought value. The popularity and actual value of the legend is in direct proportion to how well it is told and how well the truth of the principle is conveyed.

In the case of someone like Buddha or Christ, we are apparently dealing with individuals who could convey the truth with lucidity and simplicity. Because they lived the truth, they could convey it with few words and in a direct fashion. They were so good at what they did, legends abound to this day.

As a side comment, it may also interest the reader to know that there is a regular and recurring pattern behind all legends and mythologies. This pattern has been studied for ages by different cultures and mystery schools and is known by many as the "Tree of Life". It is also called the Cabala, Qabala, Kabala or Holy Kabalah. One of the best works on this subject is "The Mystical Qabala" by Dion Fortune.

The Montauk Project, as it has been told by Preston Nichols, calls on us to rally around the symbol of time and break free from its limitations. It has its own place in legend simply because it is so unique. Whether or not it is true is secondary. The concepts and penetration concerning time that both Preston and Duncan have come up with are totally foreign and alien to most of us. At the very least, they are conjuring up thoughts and avenues of consciousness that are worthy of investigation in their own right. What is of particular interest is that there is information that backs up their story. Surprisingly, this type of information is beginning to spring forth like a fountain.

It is vital that the role of legends be explained and understood because the story gets a trifle more wild and all of this should be kept in proper perspective. Some parts of this book might ring loud and clear to you as being true. Other aspects could stretch your credibility past the limit. Remember, the universe is a complex structure and our commonly accepted form of thought are limited. At the very least, we are inviting you to stretch and exercise the muscles of your thinking process with the hope it may make you stronger and more aware.

If parts of this book cannot be accepted at face value, they should be understood in the context of legend and what the bizarre meaning is behind it all. Only in this manner can one arrive at the truth behind the subject matter.

2

MONTAUK CHRONICLE

At 5:30 A.M. on October 31, 1990, I awoke suddenly and found myself looking out the window at what first appeared to be a shooting star. Instead of moving across the sky or in a downward motion, it shot up vertically. I quickly wondered if this was a UFO as meteorites do not move in such a fashion. Fifteen seconds later, a second "star" followed the exact path. There were no others. I had never seen any sort of UFO prior to this encounter.

One week later, on November 7th, I was to meet Preston Nichols. I have since been told that this sort of experience is not unusual to people who encounter him.

I met Preston as a result of a business opportunity I was interested in at the time. Without elaborating on those circumstances, I was interested in a device that he had invented. This is now known as the Biofiss and is a stereo system that is designed to balance the electromagnetic fields surrounding the body.

Two of my friends told me that I could meet Preston at a Psychotronics meeting. I showed up and met Preston briefly but soon found I would have to hear a lecture on "Earth Changes". This was a panel discussion by five different people. Both Preston and Duncan Cameron were on the panel. I sat in the audience that evening with another gentleman I would come to know: Al Bielek.

Preston spoke about orgone energy and how electromagnetic factors can affect the environment. Duncan gave first hand accounts of psychically monitoring different functions of the Earth. This was done for the U.S. Government. His role in the Philadelphia Experiment was also discussed.

I was surprised that these two speakers would say anything at all. I was aware the Government had done strange research projects, but these are things you just don't speak about. I asked them about this and Preston explained that the Government was losing control. He said they have learned over time that they can't just kill people anymore. In the past, silencing people has had a tendency to create a martyr syndrome. He pointed out the legacy of Morris K. Jessup, the man who first publicized the Philadelphia Experiment. Jessup was found dead in his car in what was sure to be a mock suicide. In many respects, his death ensured that the Philadelphia Experiment would never be forgotten.

After listening to Preston, it was obvious that the intelligence community wasn't what it used to be. Besides, Preston said that his story had been widely circulated to the point that even if he were to die of natural causes, people would suspect a hit.

As the evening continued, the Philadelphia Experiment was discussed as were many alien and UFO scenarios. All of this was new to me. I had once heard the story of the *USS Eldridge* disappearing and reappearing off the Virginia coast, but I dismissed it as nonsense. I'd never read about it. Now, I was hearing about it from people (Al and Duncan) who claimed actual involvement in the project. Their story, along with Preston's, gave the whole subject much more credibility.

The evening was quite electrically charged. Questions and answers were being fired across the room like laser darts. A lot of the information went completely over my head. It was too much to absorb. Many times during the course of the evening, the events at the Montauk Air Force Base were discussed. I asked if there was a book I could read but none existed.

Later I was told that if I wanted to see Preston's Biofiss machine, I could make an appointment with the treasurer of the Long Island Psychotronics chapter who I will refer to as Jewel. Having met her briefly, I spoke to her on the phone a few days later and found that she was leaving the organization and wanted nothing to do with it. Preston was apparently the devil and all she would say about Duncan was that he was damaged. I was given Preston's phone number and soon found myself as an observer in a goofy soap opera.

By coincidence, I ran into Jewel the following Sunday. We had common friends, and they were going to brunch. I found out later that Jewel fell flat on her face that day and had to be taken home. She was incapacitated for several days.

Preston didn't know what she was reacting to and drove all the way to her house in an attempt to console her. This didn't work. Duncan later did an extremely elaborate reading which indicated she was working undercover for another psychotronics group. I didn't know if any of this was true, but I quickly discovered that psychotronics was neither boring nor lacking in entertainment.

When I visited Preston's lab, myself and a few others were given a demonstration of the various pieces of equipment. I found the Biofiss to be interesting and therapeutic. It was very relaxing and perked up my mental awareness for a period of twenty-four hours afterwards.

During the evening, one gentleman had become excited about the idea of a book and movie for *The Montauk Project.* He asked Preston about it and was told that he could talk about it at a later date. By the end of the evening, as we walked to our cars, this gentleman did a total about face. He became afraid of the entire affair and said that he wanted to have nothing to do with it. He told me that I could write it if I wanted. Seeing him later, he was totally unwilling even to discuss the subject. His girl friend told me that she believes he was involved in the Philadelphia Experiment as he gets uneasy and clams up whenever it is mentioned.

For some reason, this subject has a way of frightening the living daylights out of those who get close to it. I also found that some people were very concerned for me when I began to write the story. Others couldn't understand why I would give any credence at all to such sinister energy as the Montauk Project. I wasn't quite sure exactly what any of these people were talking about, but it was clear that they were afraid of the energies and phenomena that Preston and Duncan dealt with on a daily basis.

I am skeptical by nature, and I didn't even know if any of the information I'd been told was true. I took it all with a grain of salt but found it high adventure and good entertainment at the very least. If the story was not true, I thought that it was better science fiction than I'd ever read.

After observing Preston's equipment and what had been left over from Montauk, it became apparent to me that the Montauk Air Force Base had served as some sort of implant station. As I explained in the introduction, I had extensively studied L. Ron Hubbard's theories on implants, some of it under his supervision. An entire book could be written about him so I have included some further information in the appendix for those who are interested.

One of his most controversial books is a title called *A History of Man*. In this book, Hubbard discusses how electronics can be used to make an entire slave society. He does not go into technical detail on the electronics but gives several samples on how beings can be snared and implanted with electronic techniques.

Whenever Hubbard was attacked, it was routine for his adversaries to quote from this book in order to show that he was "crazy". It was and is simply too far out for mainstream reporters to take seriously.

I also found the information to be extremely bizarre, but I also found that it had remarkable workability if applied under the precise procedures that were outlined. Even though I found the information useful in getting rid of psychosomatic ills (for myself and others), I could never figure out how he had discovered it. I was later told that he had acquired it from the Office of Naval Research when he was in the Navy as an intelligence officer. I don't know if this is exactly true, but it seems to fit. More about Hubbard's roots will be touched on a little later in the book.

Whatever the case, Hubbard was far ahead of his time in regards to implant research. It is highly fashionable today and is seen on tabloid TV with regularity.

Discovering Preston and the Montauk Project had completed a circle for me in regards to electronics and Hubbard. It supported some of the latter's research and answered many questions of a more subjective nature. At the very least, I was walking on familiar ground and fears that others might have were not my concern. I'd already investigated the area.

In January 1991, I attended a lecture on UFOs held by Bill Knell at a public library on Long Island. As he had been involved with the study of UFOs for some time, I waited until everyone had left and told him I might be doing a book with Preston. To my surprise, he had heard of Preston. He said that it was a great idea but that if I wanted to do a really good book, I should get Preston to tell me about ten of the other people who were involved with the Montauk Project. They could give a complete story.

A few months later, I worked out an agreement to do a book with Preston. He was surprised at what Bill had said and didn't know who I was referring to. I know now that Preston is tight lipped when necessary on the subject. Most of these people (some I have since met) do not want to talk about the project or be associated with it. I also realized that it was far easier and less time consuming to simply write Preston's version of what had happened. To do otherwise would take huge amounts of time and expense. Writing the first book has helped with the expenses, but investigating and writing about the Montauk Project has almost become a full time activity.

My above experience with Preston leads directly to a major problem when dealing with a project of this nature: it is loaded with counter-intelligence propaganda. Anything you hear on the subject has to be regarded with suspicion. People will say something one day and then deny it the next. Of course, all this indicates tremendous secrets and that somebody is hiding something. On a grander scale, we can view this situation as one manifestation of a universe that has evolved into a lower state of consciousness.

Writing the book itself was easier than dealing with the various intelligence theories. I tape recorded what Preston had to say because much of it went over my head, particularly the technical parts. I listened and transcribed every word he said and played the tapes over until I could clearly see that what he spoke of was entirely plausible. I began to dream about time travel and had experiences of a subjective nature which were quite spectacular.

Preston advised me to go out to the Montauk base with a psychic. He said it would be of interest to note what they pick up. He warned me not to go alone.

Although I know many psychics, I couldn't find one who would go out there. Some were too busy and others wanted nothing to do with it. Finally, I secured Howard Metz to go with me. Howard is a retired policeman and is very knowledgeable about psychic phenomena. He is also a pyramidologist and is mentioned in Charles Bertlitz's popular book on the Bermuda Triangle. We took the two and a half hour trip out to Montauk and left our I.D.s in the car.

As soon as one gets in the vicinity of the base, it is hard to miss the transmitter tower. It has a particularly haunting presence when you get up close, especially when the wind blows and makes subtle sounds. On a subjective basis, I found the transmitter to be quite repulsive as it elicited feelings of tragedy and horror. It seemed to stand for everything that is dire.

As we approached the base from the south end, I noticed a completely demolished building. It was the strangest demolition I had ever seen. It was not only burnt but was in total shambles. It didn't look like it had been simply blown up. Upon my return, I spoke to Preston and he told me that according to legend that was the house that Junior (the Beast) had destroyed. The legend is bizarre, but it certainly correlated with my observation of the place.

We walked around the base for a good while. I was looking for some sort of documentation or proof about the project. It was obvious the base had been active but nothing of a spectacular nature turned up. I did find some blue prints for a Sperry gyroscope. I had them in my hand when we were suddenly approached by a park ranger. He was not friendly and looked immediately at the blueprints in my hand.

"What are those?" he snapped.

"They're just blueprints," I said.

He took them hurriedly and studied them for some time. He finally looked up and asked me if I wanted them. I said no but told him I'd throw them away. They were obviously of no value, but he seemed concerned that they might be. He also insisted that we leave the base.

As we headed out, I briefly stepped into the transmitter building to verify if the torch marks Preston spoke about were there. Sure enough, they were. They were not small torch marks either. The place looked utterly devastated. It appeared that something of a highly irregular nature had gone on there.

Before we returned, we stopped for an early dinner and encountered my next odd bit of synchronicity with Montauk. Our waiter was a young man named Mirko who was from the country which was then known as Yugoslavia. Although he'd not heard of the Montauk Project, he said that he knew the curator of the Tesla Museum in Belgrade and that he was planning to translate materials that had never been put into English. He has since been unable to complete his task because of the war in that region. I found this whole meeting rather odd as most people don't even know about Tesla, let alone have an intimate understanding of his work. What were the chances of my meeting such a person at Montauk?

A short while after my return from Montauk, I was at a gathering at Howard's house. There, I was approached by a man who I will refer to as Mr. X. He wanted to know how the book was coming along. I found his interest to be quite odd. He took me aside and told me in private that he had been involved in the negotiations to secure the Montauk Chair. Upon relaying this story to my wife, she told me that he must have been negotiating with aliens. I hadn't thought about it, but her observation seemed to fit in with the story. He also mentioned that he had managed a very sizable portfolio for the Montauk group.

Mr. X wanted to tell me about his involvement, and we arranged a meeting at a diner in Amityville. There, he informed me that he had lots of contacts on both sides of the project. In other words, he had friends who wanted the information to get out. There were others in the military industrial complex who didn't want it discussed at all. He said that he was sort of in the middle and that the whole subject causes him considerable anxiety. He backed off on his plan to discuss the subject and said that things had gotten too hot for him to say anything.

He was clearly frightened on some level. At times, his conversation seemed calculated to scare me. I believe that he had some sort of "Montauk programs" operating during the conversation. Something was activating his speech and behavior that wasn't himself. He's actually quite a nice person and has a keen intellect.

The above behavior is symptomatic of what I call "the Montauk personality". People who have been involved in the project have distinctly different personalities. This does not appear to be ordinary schizophrenia but would seem to be programming of some sort. The personality change seems to kick in only when the subject of UFOs, mind control or Montauk itself is brought up.

Mr. X then proceeded to explain various aspects of what he believed got Montauk started in the first place. That will be talked about later on. He was definitely a knowledgeable individual and was apparently a double agent on some level. I later did a minor background check on Mr. X and discovered that many aspects of his life pointed in the direction of a true experience connected with Montauk.

Meeting Mr. X was just one more incident that made the Montauk story more credible in my own mind. I have since been slowly acclimated to various others who claim involvement in the project. There are also others who won't discuss or admit anything.

After my meeting with Mr. X, events became a little more serious. I was now having dreams of dark entities and Men in Black. It seemed someone was attempting to frighten me by amplified psychic means. It didn't work. Threats of a psychic nature are just threats. If they wanted me to stop my work, they were going to have to try something in person. That way, I hoped, I could catch someone in the act and it would give proof to the story.

The next event of import occurred when speaking on the phone to a psychic healer I know. She was having dinner with another psychic. His name was Michael, and I had met him only briefly in the past. I told her to tell him about the book I was doing.

Michael called me up almost immediately. He said that she didn't have to say anything and that he had picked up what was going on as soon as she had put down the phone. He said that there was a government agent who wanted to nail me. He gave a complete description and said that I should lay off the book for a couple of years.

I was not about to lay off the book. Shortly thereafter, I was washing the car when a middle-age man pulled up and watched me for the longest time. I was aware of his presence in the car but didn't know he was watching me. This was pointed out to me by my wife who was watching him from the house. He finally drove off.

After another week, when I was on vacation, a message was left on my phone at 3:00 A.M. A woman's voice said, "You know who I am. Stay out of it."

I had no idea who it was. There was no possibility that it was a wrong number. They had called on my business phone and first had to hear an entire taped message referring to my business.

Up to this point, I hadn't told Preston about any of these events. At our next meeting I told him that there were some people who didn't want me to write this book.

He looked at me quizzically and said "What do you mean?"

I began to tell him the story of the "government agent". I'd hardly said anything, but as soon as the term "government agent" came out of my mouth, he interrupted me.

He said, "That's already been taken care of."

"What do you mean?" I asked.

Preston told me that Duncan had gotten a similar reading two weeks earlier that indicated a government agent was after me. He then called one of his friends at a highly placed government agency and told him to tell the CIA to lay off of me. If they didn't, he would publish secret papers that they didn't want published.

Up to now, I'd had reason to be afraid but hadn't reacted. Preston's comments shocked me because there was no way he could have made it up. He'd reacted immediately and couldn't have concocted anything that fast. I also remembered that Duncan had approached me a week earlier and asked what would happen to the book if either Preston or myself suddenly died. I'd thought it was a hypothetical question. Now, I knew that Duncan was inquiring with regard to his own reading. He was also kind enough not to try and alarm me.

I was not so much shocked for my life. I was surprised

that Duncan's reading had correlated exactly with that of the other psychic. It brought home the point to me that this was not a joke and that the intelligence community took it very seriously. Prior to that point, I had considered it a highly entertaining science fiction story that was somewhat true.

Preston had also told me about the secret papers previously. He had actually acquired them by happenstance when he purchased some surplus electronic equipment. The Government had supposedly found out about it and asked him not to publish the information. He agreed for his own reasons at the time, but now it appeared that someone was trying to interfere with the publication of *The Montauk Project*. He was not about to let his book be suppressed.

Since this conversation with Preston, nothing of a threatening nature has occurred. The strange dreams also stopped.

In addition to the above, there is another series of events which I think are noteworthy to add. These began as the first manuscript neared completion. I asked Preston to dig up all his photographs concerning the project. This required a bit of hounding as he is not the most organized person and always has plenty of other things to do.

One day, I went into his area and found his work place completely cleaned up. He pointed to the couch at a pile of photos and said to take a look. I was totally surprised to find a photo of the beast. He'd never told me he had a photo that good, and he was extremely casual about it. It wasn't a big deal to him, but it was amazing to me. I'd heard a lot about the beast and heard about photos, but this one was pretty convincing.

I asked him several questions about it, but he didn't have too many answers. The beast had not been there when the photo was taken. It was just bizarre phenomena. He couldn't account for it. I, of course, wondered if it were some sort of prank. I asked him who took the photo, and he said it was done by Jan Brice. Preston then asked me if I would like to speak to him. I said yes, and Preston called him up and introduced me over the phone. We discussed the photograph, and it was apparent that Preston was not at all playing a hoax. In fact, Jan said that he had attempted a lot of supernatural photography over the years, but this was the only result he'd ever gotten. He wasn't trying to capture the beast, he was just trying to capture a picture of a bunker.

I spoke to Jan several times after that. He confided to me that he wasn't sure the beast was what Preston thought it was. He just couldn't account for the phenomena. He told me that he had worked as an astrophysicist and had worked out some of the early lunar trajectories before man had gone to the moon. He dropped out of the scientific community and joined a monastery for eleven years. Now, he was a writer and had just completed his first book, *Secrets of Consciousness*.

Jan said that he had mixed feelings about Preston. He told me a story of how Preston had called up one of his friends complaining about a bomb being in his lab. Preston claimed to have taken the bomb across the street, departing before it blew up. Jan's friend visited Preston the next day but found no visible evidence. To this day, Preston is not sure what happened. He thought it could be time phenomena, but he definitely remembered the bomb.

Jan was quick to point out that in spite of this incident, he had seen Preston talk to people who had been involved in projects like Montauk and would know the strangest things about them. He'd help them pull their memories, and there was no doubting that Preston had special knowledge and uncanny ability. He also said Preston was amazingly brilliant.

For his help, we had decided to put Jan's name in the acknowledgments, and we were going to give him special mention on the title page as a photographer. At the last minute, after I'd told him about my experience with Duncan and Michael picking up psychic warnings about me, he begged off. He didn't want his name mentioned in the book at all.

I was amused at his fear because he was far less of a target than I was. He said he didn't want his room ransacked by someone looking for photos or negatives. We left him out according to his wishes. He also told me that we'd see if I survived the first printing of *The Montauk Project.*

Jan died within a couple of months of that last conversation. Although he was connected to the United States Psychotronics Association, we have no evidence to suggest that he was rubbed out. A pervasive rumor was circulated that he'd died of food poisoning. According to Jan's girl friend, the autopsy indicated a heart attack as the cause of death. She refuted the food poisoning rumor. If that is true, it raises minor suspicions. Inducing heart attacks is a common trick. The Mafia used to have a reputation of lacing apple pies so as to induce cardiac arrest. Personally, I don't understand what motivation anyone would have to kill him. The photographs he took are suggestive but are not conclusive proof of anything. The only other questions would be: did he know something else?

In any event, Jan was a great person and a dynamic speaker. We have chosen to dedicate this book to him.

3

MONTAUK — THE PROOF?

I would like to prove the Montauk story as much as anyone. By that, I mean irrefutable documentation that would stand up to any inspection. I am convinced that there was a project out at Montauk that was of a top secret nature. That it included mind control, I am certain. The time aspect is the most difficult to establish although Preston's theories and memories, along with those of Duncan and Al Bielek, are quite enlightening.

Proof does not come easily. I liken it to the analogy of a father who abuses his entire family. The father, of course, denies that he does anything wrong. The family are so cowed that they absolutely deny any wrong doing by their patriarch. This type of behavior is also seen in the movie "The Wizard of Oz" when the witch's entire army cheers after Dorothy throws water and melts her. Prior to this, they were all profusely bowing down.

It is totally understandable that people can be afraid, especially if they consider their lives are at stake. But, I believe it is important that the whole matter be put in proper perspective. Any time someone gets scared or hides evidence, they are paying tribute to the bogus authority that is behind the Montauk Project.

We said in the first book that there are varying degrees of proof. This chapter will deal with actual examples and experiences that will serve to establish that the Montauk Project, in some form, took place.

One of our strongest pieces of hard evidence in *The Montauk Project* was the section on the radiosonde and how it was used to modify the weather. We received one review on the book by a gentleman who gave it a fairly nice review, except that he refuted the data about the radiosondes. He said it was off base from his personal experience. He did work on radiosondes, but what he doesn't tell us is that he worked in a top secret capacity. He signed nondisclosure forms and it would be his "duty" to hold the government line. He had to deny it. It is always interesting when your critics make false criticism and that is just one example.

After the book was published, I did try to dig up some information that would corroborate Preston's information. First, I spoke with Dick White. He is the head of the Montauk Historical Society and is extremely knowledgeable about Montauk's history. He is very friendly and was most helpful. When I told him about the book and gave him a brief rendition of the story, he told me that he'd have thought I was crazy except that there was a fellow in a tavern the night before who was talking about a documentary to be done on the Philadelphia Experiment. He had some idea of what I was talking about, but it was simply too far out for him to easily grasp in a single phone conversation.

Dick did have some interesting stories though. When I asked him about animals storming Montauk, he did remember two deer running into the town with one crashing into a phone booth and the other falling and sliding into the doorway of an establishment. He thought it was strange but that it could possibly be the result of a dog chasing the deer. No dog was observed though.

He also spoke of an incident in 1972 when he drove a friend to the inner gate of the Montauk Base. His friend worked there and was allowed to enter but the guard pointed a gun at Dick's windshield right in the direction of his three year old son. Dick asked him to leave the kid alone. The guard subsequently pointed the gun at him and demanded to know what he was doing there. Dick and his son got away unscathed, but this is incredibly strange behavior for what was purported to be a simple FAA (Federal Aviation Administration) radar installation. It was also an innocent mistake at worst on Dick's part. The guard's irrational behavior indicates that something of a very sensitive nature was taking place. The entire incident also suggests that the guard could have been programmed in some fashion.

Dick then gave me the phone number of some technicians he knew of who had worked at the base. I was able to get hold of one who I will refer to as Ken. This gentleman said he had not heard of the Philadelphia Experiment and that he had retired in about '73.

Asking Ken if anything strange ever went on at the base, he wanted to know what I meant by strange. I asked if he ever saw any guns around the base or anything like that. He denied it emphatically. I then asked if there were any type of guns out there whatsoever. He continued to deny it until I told him the above story by Dick White. He then changed his tenor and said, "Well, of course, there were guns. It was a high security area because of the radar and it had to be protected." I had caught him in a definite lie and I knew I couldn't trust anything he said. He did admit to a brand new computer being installed in about '73 just as he was about to retire. This is the same date Preston had given for the computer change.

There was another odd report from a contractor. This man had a gardener working for him who would be routinely shocked whenever he hit a piece of metal in the ground while working at houses near the base. This is evidence of a highly charged electric field in the vicinity of the base.

Things took a different turn when I spoke with Dan Rattiner. He is the editor and publisher of *Dan's Papers*, a long established local newspaper on the East End of Long Island. He also publishes the local *Montauk Pioneer*.

Dan was very courteous although he was too ready to challenge the information in the book. He did remember geese storming the town once, but he disagreed strongly with the stories about snow in August. He had temperature recordings in his paper over the years and wouldn't vouch for any weather that unusual. (Preston's reports were not from his own observations but were from stories he'd heard from kids on the beach. He also got a report from someone who claimed to have kept a weather log on the Montauk Base. It was hearsay. Interestingly, just before this book went to press, we got one report from a woman who said their indeed had been snow in the summer.)

Although I had not read his paper, Dan informed me that he liked to write hoaxes. He said they were obvious hoaxes. I eventually got my hands on the paper and found that he did indeed write some very amusing articles. He told me that he would occasionally write about a man who worked at a station on the east end of Long Island who worked in a weather control station. This was part of a network of weather control stations across the country. This was all pure fiction and good fun according to him.

While Dan eventually did review the book, he remained skeptical. He did help the sales of the book though, and we thank him for that. Some of my friends have suggested that he is a plant who would secretly work against any promulgation of the Montauk story. I do not have any evidence to suggest that, but I have met other individuals from Montauk who I believe to be complicit (not necessarily on a conscious basis) with a cover up concerning the Montauk Air Force Base.

After speaking with the above people, I decided to venture out to Montauk once again. This time I would go with Maria Fix, a world class psychic. Maria is a clairvoyant who can find lost keys and that sort of thing. She's very good and people fly from across the world just to get a reading. Maria is also consulted by the police frequently to help solve difficult cases by psychic means. Up to this point, she had not met Preston or Duncan but had been independently investigating Montauk from a psychic point of view.

On my way to Maria's house, which was in the direction of Montauk from my home, I saw a bright flash in the sky and noticed a UFO that was big, reddish orange and dipping. I could only see part of the craft which disappeared very quickly. It seemed to be in an opening through a distortion of some sort in the atmosphere. In some weird way, the craft seemed to be acknowledging that they knew I was on my way. I went to Maria's and we proceeded to go to Montauk.

Maria drove and we first went to the Montauk State parking lot for the lighthouse. She pulled up a few yards in front of the parking attendant's booth (it costs $3.00 to park in the lot) and said that she was going to create an illusion. She then approached the booth very slowly and stopped. There was an elderly lady in the booth. The lady robotically turned her head in the opposite direction, and we slipped on by. Whether this was a psychic trick or good luck is open to debate, but Maria did call her shot. She is quite good at this sort of thing and frankly she has to be. She supports three children through her psychic practice.

I had taken my video camcorder and was taking shots of the lighthouse and of the base from a distance. We obtained permission to go to the base and walked around with myself getting as much footage as possible. I made a direct line for the transmitter building. I was eager to see this because Preston had told me to check for new cables he'd heard had been put in there. This would indicate the underground was active. Having briefly visited the transmitter building on my first trip to Montauk, I had seen huge torch marks and indications of some sort of explosions. I didn't have a flashlight then but now I did and was hoping to get a better look. Unfortunately, the building was locked up, but there was new cable leading to it. A huge steel door had been put over the front and rear openings. It looked as if they were trying to prevent a military assault or the like.

Maria then pointed to an area less than 100 yards from the transmitter building where she had seen a stealth aircraft on a previous visit. It had been flying close to the ground before it suddenly disappeared. We searched around some more, and I continued to video tape the area. All in all, I was disappointed that the transmitter building was closed and that I hadn't turned up anything that appeared to be significant.

The only strange happening that I noticed occurred as we were driving home. I sensed what I could almost hear as a voice. It wasn't a voice though. Whatever "it" was gave me a message that I will never forget. It said, "Don't ever come back here again." I do not ordinarily hear voices. Of course, this could have been my subconscious mind. But if communication is possible by psychotronics,

I would guess that someone was trying to tell me something. I would not return to Montauk for almost six months. Upon returning home, I viewed about 20 minutes of video footage that I'd taken. I didn't notice anything that I considered to be unusual or paranormal. My wife noticed that there was a dot in the viewfinder of the camcorder. She was upset at me as she thought I'd broken it. I didn't know what the dot was, but I was entirely certain that I'd not dropped or otherwise mishandled the camera.

Six weeks after the trip to Montauk, my wife noticed that the video camera was missing. It had been placed next to a portable TV which rested on shelving. I looked in all the usual places and realized that it was gone. I then said that I wanted to see if the Montauk footage was missing; then we would know if it was an inside job. Sure enough, the Montauk footage was missing. It had been on the opposite side of the television.

This was obviously not a routine burglary. If it was, they could have taken far more equipment than a camcorder. There was much more there for the grabbing. Also, why would they bother with worthless tapes? There was no sign of any break-in. It is also virtually impossible to enter my house without leaving a trace. It is white and very clean and the backyard could not have been penetrated without turning up some mud.

We later found out that the battery pack was also taken. It was in another room and was totally hidden under a table and papers. This fact led me to conclude that the equipment might have been teleported by some sort of advanced technology. It could be that the equipment which had been taken was all witnessed to Montauk as it had just been at the base. ("Witness" is an occult term which refers to a sympathetic correspondence. For example, the people who were cursed as a result of unsealing King Tut's tomb were "witnessed" to the curse.) I called Preston and explained the circumstances. He said the dot in the viewfinder was the result of a bad video cell. This was probably due to the distortion in the electromagnetic field at Montauk. He reminded me of a video he'd shown me where people were taking pictures of the Montauk underground and were getting intermittent but consistent interference with their video equipment.

It is obviously impossible to prove that my video camera was teleported, but it was definitely taken in a manner that I feel is extremely suspicious. Preston thought that they might want the camera as it was smoking gun proof of a distortion in the field out there. This is still an unresolved mystery.

On August 12, 1992, Preston held an open house at Space-Time Labs. He invited anyone who wanted to come from the Long Island Psychotronics Chapter. He had put together the FRR-224 receiver. This was the receiver he had purchased from Dr. Rinehart (who was thought to be John von Neumann, the technical genius behind the Montauk Project). It is an extremely sensitive receiver, and he wanted to see what he could pick up. The August 12 date was significant as that is the anniversary of the Philadelphia Experiment and also the culmination of the Montauk Project.

I didn't expect much to occur, but I thought I'd better be there to record anything of interest that might happen. It was a quiet evening in the middle of summer and only Duncan and one other gentleman showed up besides Preston. We listened to all sorts of ear piercing frequencies but we all had to leave the radio room after a while. The sounds were not conducive to a peaceful state of mind. Preston continued to fiddle with the instruments. No amount of feedback or different frequencies seems to unsettle him.

As the evening passed, I had some interesting conversations with Duncan. Then, two Montauk psychics showed up. These are two individuals who remember working in the Montauk Chair. They went into the radio room, sat down and seemed to concentrate on the various frequencies. Duncan explained that they were just trying to pick up on a frequency that they could synchronize with and "trip out" on. In other words, certain psycho-active frequencies would promulgate various responses in the psychic. He would then receive information or just experience communication of some sort from an unconventional source. They obviously had experienced some sort of indoctrination in this particular technique. This was revelatory to me and it's why I chose to mention it. While I felt that I could indeed try this technique and be somewhat successful at it, I had no inclination whatsoever to do it. It seemed too abrasive for my personal taste.

Another interesting development occurred in September. I received a phone call from a friend of mine, who I will refer to as John. A friend of his had read the book and wanted to go to Montauk with me. The man was a professional photographer and wanted to take some photographs with his infrared equipment.

I was not eager to go back to Montauk but before I could even respond to the request, I was called again by John. He said that his friend had already made the trip and that I could come over and pick up the photos in an envelope the next morning. I phoned the next dat, but was told not to bother. John's friend had gotten so excited over the photos that he decided to go down to Washington and show them to his brother in the Navy. The brother worked in the electronics area.

John got word from his friend upon his return. He was told that he'd have the pictures the very next day. John was eager to see them but hadn't up to this point. The friend never showed up and stopped returning John's calls. This was odd to say the least as they were good friends and this sort of behavior had not occurred before.

John's other friends and myself all speculated on what had happened. Some thought that the person might want money for the pictures but John and I doubted that. We thought there was something of an unusual nature that was on the infrared photos but we just didn't know what.

While these events were taking place, Preston called and asked me to visit him. Some new developments had taken place, and he didn't want to mention them over the phone.

Upon arriving at his shop, he showed me a vast array of video equipment. He had gotten a call a few days earlier from a friend and was told of an auction that was to take place at Venus Scientific. The company was apparently bankrupt and they were selling the stock. Preston was able to acquire literally tens of thousands worth of equipment for $70.00. The equipment just happened to be night vision equipment, both infrared and ultraviolet. A lot of it was spare parts, but very valuable to a skilled professional. I suggested that it might have been a set up. I told Preston that the individual who made the call to him was probably connected to Montauk. He thought that was possible and explained that strange things like this happen to him all the time. Someone wanted him to have the equipment.

Preston subsequently took this equipment and took infrared video pictures of the Montauk base. The video revealed what were either thought forms rising from the transmitter area or a release of heat from same. Either way, it is a major oddity as a heat release would indicate the installation was active underground. Preston later took the infrared equipment to upstate New York and reported that he was able to visibly see UFOs with this equipment. Al Bielek was with him and confirmed the report.

When I heard all this, it occurred to me that John's friend might have recorded a UFO over Montauk. I spoke to John about this, and he mentioned that his friend had gone to the Norfolk Navy Base in Virginia. I was earlier told that he'd gone to Washington. Norfolk is significant for two reasons. One, that is where the *USS Eldridge* reportedly shifted to in 1943. Two, the Norfolk Navy Base is reported to a be a hot seat of top secret information.

As time progressed, John's friend never did come through with the photos. He'd call or show up but there was always some excuse. After about six months, we got word that the man's house had been burned down completely. Only the chimney stump was left standing. Arson was suspected as young boys had been seen in the vacant lot that was adjacent to the house. Further investigation by the fire department revealed that an accelerant had been used. This ruled out any likelihood of the fire being an accident. It is also unlikely that the boys would use an accelerant in carrying out ordinary juvenile delinquency. In fact, the accelerant was so high powered that the entire house was gone by the time the fire department arrived. What exactly happened is still a mystery at this writing. John can no longer call his friend as the phone was burned, but he did receive one call from the man since the fire. He was told not to believe anything he heard about the fire. It would all be explained at a later date. John said that his friend's behavior totally changed after he became actively interested in the Montauk phenomena.

The next unusual circumstance was a phone call from a kid who said he had some information for me. He had been out to the base after reading the book and had turned up some papers. I wasn't about to go driving off immediately and possibly walk into a trap. I told him to keep them in a safe place and I would call back in a few weeks. He then began to sound a little frightened. I told him not to worry because Preston and I had written an entire book and nothing had happened to us. I phoned him a few weeks later and was told that no such person lived there. I was given several runarounds. Finally, his mother asked if I was the one who wrote *The Montauk Project*. I confirmed that, but she said that the person who had called was a neighbor and didn't live there. I finally concluded that the kid must have given me an assumed name and wanted no part of it. He also had a friend whom I'd spoken with who also turned suddenly uncooperative.

An even odder occurrence happened when I received a call from my friend Mary. She had been talking with her friend Ivey, an occupational therapist at a nearby psychiatric facility. Ivey remembered taking care of a man who had been a top scientist. This scientist claimed he had worked on a project that included a ray gun that made people invisible. The staff view was that the man was nuts but Ivey said no. He didn't act crazy but just claimed this unusual experience. She argued about it with her supervisor, but the supervisor simply said that he must be nuts. After all, he was in an institution!

One of Ivey's fellow therapists was a part timer who also worked in the U.S. Army. This man told her that the scientist had worked out at Montauk on a project called NORDOR (spelling could be incorrect). I sent Ivey a book and asked her to contact the man from the Army on my behalf. Upon calling her two weeks later her number had been disconnected and no trace of her has turned up yet. I believe she wants to stay away from any involvement in this investigation.

I later found out from my friend Kenn Arthur that NORDOR was a top secret defense project. Although he hadn't heard about the invisibility factor, he said that it apparently had to do with radar.

Another interesting story unfolded when Madalyn Suozzo visited Long Island from California and showed up at a Psychotronics meeting one evening. She has worked in the healing arts for twenty years and practices Regenesis, a technique that regenerates cellular tissue by working with the original blue print (on a psychic cellular level) for the human body. Madalyn returned to her home in California and read the book. After reading it, she recalled some strange experiences while she was at Montauk as a teenager in 1973.

Madalyn had studied yoga and healing for a couple of years but had only had a couple of psychic experiences up to that point. When she had gone to Montauk to join her friends and look for a waitressing job in the summer of '73, she began to hear voices in the wind and began to experience different psychic phenomena.

Perhaps the most spectacular occurence concerned a wino fisherman who shared a house with Madalyn and her friends. The fisherman was an interesting man and had different books on psychic phenomena. He lived upstairs but had an odd schedule and was seldom there. After reading one of his books, Madalyn had an incredibly strong clairvoyant vision of Jesus Christ. She has since experienced clairvoyance on a somewhat regular basis but nothing else has ever come through that strong or appeared so clearly. In fact, Madalyn said that her perceptions and experiences were magnified the entire summer. All of this would correspond to the mind amplification techniques that were being used at Montauk.

One day the wino fisherman and four of Madalyn's

friends were in the house together. Madalyn told him that she was interested in his books when he suddenly looked her straight in the eye and said, "You and I are different from these other people".

Madalyn recounts what happened next.

"He then waved his hand to make a partition so as to divide us from the rest of the group. The light on our side of the room became lighter and the light on the other side became darker. He had made a statement and then backed it up with a demonstration."

Since hearing this story originally, I now know Madalyn well enough to know that she doesn't make up stories. It is also interesting to note that the summer of '73 corresponds to the ten year biorhythm of Montauk (which was 12 August 1983). According to what Preston has been told, the twenty year biorhythm was considered the stronger factor but the ten year biorhythms are potent as well.

There are several more such anecdotes that corroborate that a Montauk Project of some sort did exist. In fact, there are more than I could remember or easily put down on paper. Although these experiences are entirely legitimate, none of the information presented herein is designed or intended to constitute objective court of law style proof. That is an entirely different project that someone else might want to take up further down the road. But these various experiences and stories do reveal an interesting pattern that warrants further investigation. Ultimately, the only valid proof can be measured in terms of experience and there is plenty more of that. This entire subject involves a scenario of developing consciousness and what you have read thus far is only the beginning. The rest of this book will reveal more.

4

MONTAUK, THE OCCULT AND THORN E.M.I.

There is an amazing occult connection to the Montauk Project and the next part of our investigation will take us into that arena.* Later in the book, we will return to more corroborative information about the project itself.

Anyone who seriously studies the occult will sooner or later encounter the work of Aleister Crowley. This in not an accident. In fact, he designed it that way by plastering his name in any conceivable way so as to achieve recognition. For those who are not familiar with this man already, read Appendix B which gives a synopsis of his life and philosophy.

Crowley was very influential and arguably near the peak of his magical career when he opted to take a "magical retirement" to Montauk Point during the summer of 1918. (A magical retirement consists of a withdrawal from normal mundane matters to work on "matters magical".)

---

* According to Preston, the paranormal was studied and used profusely at Montauk, not dissimilar to way the Nazis' used their Occult Bureau. Most of the personnel used at Montauk had an interest or aptitude for occult matters. This included secretaries, typists and the usual mundane jobs that are required to keep a base running. It is also presumed that these personnel had additional duties of a more esoteric nature.

What exactly transpired there remains a mystery to this day, but this book will reveal a very mysterious connection between Crowley and Montauk.

I first became aware of Crowley's association with Montauk when Preston had informed me that he remembered an earlier life as Preston B. Wilson. In that life, he had allegedly been the twin brother of Marcus Wilson who is thought to be Duncan Cameron in this incarnation. They were known as the Wilson brothers and manufactured the first electronic instruments in Great Britain. These were crude instruments which monitored electric pulsations.

The Wilson brothers were associated with the Crowley family as friends and as business partners. Together, the two families shared a business interest in a corporation that would later merge with several other companies in the 1920's. This conglomeration would eventually be known as Thorn E.M.I., one of the largest electronics firms in the United Kingdom. They also have a famous entertainment division which includes music and video publishing. Interestingly, Thorn E.M.I. is the company that distributed the movie *The Philadelphia Experiment*.

The above information concerning the Wilsons and Thorn has to be considered legend at this point because not all of it has yet been confirmed by normal physical universe means (documentation, etc.). It is mentioned for two reasons. One, as you will discover later in this book, the Wilson connection has received the most amazing corroboration. Second, we hope that by publishing the Crowley-Wilson-Thorn connection that we will arrive at further answers. The legend will also be of interest to most readers.

The Thorn connection is admittedly abstract but it is integral to the legend of the Wilson Brothers. The story also gnaws at us and won't go away. It begins in approximately 1986 when Preston received a call from a man who identified himself as William Berkelely, the historian for Thorne, E.M.I. At that time, Thorn had an office in New York City. The historian was from the parent company in England and arranged to visit Preston in person.

Upon their meeting, the historian wanted to know why the name Preston B. Nichols appeared in their archives. Preston didn't know anything about it but was curious. Preston was then shown a photograph of himself that was allegedly taken in the late 1800's. The Preston in the photo was presumably from the future as he had grayer hair and looked older. While this photograph has to be considered legend, it should be noted that there are a few others who claim to have seen this photograph.

The photograph consisted of Preston Wilson, Marcus Wilson, Preston Nichols and a fourth unnamed individual (some have speculated that it was Crowley). The historian told Preston that two of the individuals were the Wilsons. He also explained that the Thorn company was originally connected to the Crowley and Wilson families.

Preston's mother, who has read various books about Aleister Crowley, said she remembered reading about the Wilson brothers in one of Crowley's books. She recalled that the Wilson and Crowley families were involved in some enterprise. Unfortunately, she didn't remember the specific book and no one has yet been able to turn up a Wilson in the literature on Crowley. Also of interest is that one of Duncan's readings indicated that Preston's mother was a Wilson in a previous life.

This entire story takes another twist when we consider that Thorn E.M.I. is considered by some to have been involved in producing the movie *The Philadelphia Experiment*. This information comes from a childhood friend of Preston's who we will refer to as Mark Knight. While this is a controversial claim, there is no denying that the Thorn name appears on the video cassette packaging. Mark also claims to be the actor Mark Hamill who appeared as Luke Skywalker in the *Star Wars* trilogy. Preston will not officially identify him as Mark Hamill as he thinks he may be a look alike. It is also interesting to note that I have received totally independent information that Mark and Duncan Cameron used to be good friends. Based upon this and a private file I have seen, I believe Mark Hamill and Mark Knight to be one and the same.

There is also another important point to consider about Mark Hamill. When he was married at the height of his fame, the *National Enquirer* ran an article about him and his new bride. It just happened to drop the information that his father was a retired U.S. Naval intelligence officer.

Mark Knight not only looks exactly like the aforesaid actor, but he remembers working at Montauk while the project was in full force. In any event, he was instrumental in getting Preston work as a sound engineer for *The Empire Strikes Back*. More significantly, he claims to be the actual producer of the movie *The Philadelphia Experiment*. It is believed he did it in conjunction with Thorne E.M.I. and through shell companies. He was not listed in the credits as he wanted to keep his identity secret.

Mark was not alone in his plot to reveal the story of the *U.S.S. Eldridge*. His brother is known as Peter Knight, also a childhood friend of Preston's. He played in a band known as Gary Puckett and the Union Gap in the 1960's but is perhaps better known for his role in the Moody Blues *Days of Future Past* album. He was the conductor of the orchestra and his name appears on the cover. Of more interest to this story, Peter supposedly sat on the Board of Directors for Thorn E.M.I. It is not known what exactly his role was but he is thought to have played a significant part.

Peter is no longer affiliated with the company and when last seen by Preston (in the U.S.), he claimed to be on the run from the intelligence community.

According to this legend, the movie was released to theaters across the U.S. but was pulled by court order at the behest of government officials. Thorn E.M.I. supposedly went to court and got the original order rescinded. It has been speculated that Thorn's foreign status helped immeasurably in that they could not easily be intimidated by American authorities. But by then, it was too late. The movie was a disaster financially and Mark claimed that he was nearly bankrupt. Fortunately, it could then be released as a video for broad distribution. Mark was then able to get his initial investment back.

Al Bielek has made countless attempts to verify this aspect of the story but has come up empty handed so far. He did talk to a man who claimed to be Mark Hamill's agent but this person denied the entire affair. I did get a bit luckier than Al. I received a phone call from Howard Barkway in England. He is the president of Bellevue Books (which distributes *The Montauk Project* in the U.K.) and offered to do some digging on the Thorn E.M.I. connection. Howard met with a very uncooperative bureaucracy at their headquarters but did find out a little bit. According to his research, Thorn bought the rights to the movie through different shell companies. One of these was housed in the same lot as Pinewood Studios. This is noteworthy because that is the same studio where *The Empire Strikes Back* was shot. It doesn't prove but backs up the possibility of a Mark Hamill connection.

Whatever the case is with all of this, it is a fact that *The Philadelphia Experiment* was critically acclaimed but didn't last but a short time in the theaters. If none of this story is true, it would seem at least a little odd that a movie could fold totally at the box office after receiving excellent reviews and then do blockbuster sales and be quite popular as a video.

In Al Bielek's attempt to verify Thorn's connection to all this, he spoke to Douglas Curtis, who is listed on the credits as the producer of the movie *The Philadelphia Experiment*. According to Al's account, Curtis denies any involvement by Thorn E.M.I. His story was that the movie did not do well in the box office and was sold to Thorn E.M.I. for video distribution. The movie then sat on the shelf for a considerable period of time before being released as a video.

Curtis's story could easily be accepted at face value, except that the movie he produced went beyond the bounds of the normal Philadelphia Experiment story. Prior to the movie, no mention of full blown time travel had existed in the literature on the subject. The movie introduced a connection to the future from the 1943 experiment. This was not only a novel idea, but the future year that was reached in the movie was 1984, just one year away from 1983. They didn't go to Montauk but ended up in the desert. Allegedly, the date and location were changed so not to rub the story in the nose of the Government.

The movie also has the time travelers go to a base where they are befriended (to some degree) by a scientist much like John von Neumann. Additionally, the cold spells that one of the time travellers felt are similar to those experienced by Al Bielek.

All of this becomes interesting when we consider that Duncan had independently arrived at a similar story line through psychic readings and by recalling his own circumstances. Consequently, when Preston and Duncan eventually saw the movie, they were intrigued as to how the writers could have obtained such a close approximation to what they recognized as the actual story line.

Two possible explanations came to the surface almost immediately. One was came from a person who told Preston off the record that Doug Curtis had somehow acquired the actual government file on the project (though Curtis officially denies it). The other explanation came from another source and said that Thorne E.M.I. had acquired a video tape in VHS format during the 1970's that revealed key parts of the story. As VHS did not come about until the 1980's, the tape wasn't played for years. It had apparently been sent from the future. It is also possible that if such a video existed, it could have contributed to the file that Doug Curtis allegedly possessed.

Things took yet another turn when Preston and I were doing a radio show on KOA in Denver. A gentleman called who claimed to be Mike Janover, the screenwriter for *The Philadelphia Experiment*. He'd never heard about any of the Montauk information and was quite surprised. He left his phone number with the producer and I called him afterwards.

Mike said that it was his idea to put time travel into the movie. He said the movie had been rewritten about eight times before he was hired to do the job. Prior to his involvement, the scripts were trying to depict a deep and dark secret not unlike the Watergate scandal, but he didn't understand what that was all about. After all, what is so bad and secretive about a relatively few people being killed, maimed or otherwise damaged when there were thousands upon thousands dying in World War II? He said that he personally loves the idea of time travel as a subject and used that to spice up the script.

Preston wondered if this really was the Mike Janover who wrote the script or if he was a plant that had called in to throw us off. I think he was the real Mike Janover, but

I have no way of knowing that for sure.

Mike told me some other curious information. He said that while he was at an eating establishment in Fort Collins, Colorado, he got to talking with someone there. When he mentioned that he'd recently scripted *The Philadelphia Experiment*, the person mentioned that they knew Carlos Allende*.

Mike thought this was a very remarkable coincidence. Not only was Allende intimately involved with the original Philadelphia Experiment, but he has made a habit of being hard to find. He would chronically make mysterious appearances and disappearances. But this wasn't the only coincidence Mike would experience. One week later he met a man whose father was the commander of the *U.S.S. Eldridge*! This man had served as commander after the experiments had been completed.

He also told me that Orion pictures took a strong interest in initially financing the picture. They backed away, but I mention it as Orion will fit in later in this story. 20th Century Fox was involved for a while and Mike remembered that they had a whole file full of documentation on the project. This backs up what Preston had heard independently about Doug Curtis having a file.

Finally, New World Pictures picked it up and the final O.K. for the picture was given by Bob Rehme who now heads the Academy of Motion Picture Arts and Sciences. This man is obviously a very important political power in Hollywood and his connections are probably quite intriguing in themselves.

---

* For those who do not know, Carlos Allende was the man who broke the original Philadelphia Experiment story by writing to Morris K. Jessup. At the time, Allende was reported as working as a ranch hand in the local area. He is currently in a nursing home and has requested to see Al Bielek but the meeting has not taken place yet. This is an interesting development because he has avoided Al for decades. It will eventually be reported in *The Pulse*.

It is also noteworthy to mention that Mike indicated that he worked with a special science advisor on the script. Unfortunately, he wouldn't give me the name of the man. This man was reportedly quite knowledgeable and could have possibly been a plant of some sort.

Mike told me what appears to be an honest and interesting story. If we assume he's truthful, there are two other possibilities that could be at play. One is that he had involvement in the project itself and was writing from his own submerged memories. The script process had gone through a labyrinth of decision makers before it got to him. Maybe he was purposely selected to write it. The other possibility is that he tuned into it simply by exercising his own creative process. He is already a creative person and a successful writer who loves time travel. In fact, he told me that he had scripted a series called *The Time Police* (this show has yet to see the light of day).

All of this information opens the door to an intriguing consideration. The very concept of Time Police implies a manipulation and monitoring of time itself. Where did the concept come from? Mike says he made it up, just like the script for *The Philadelphia Experiment*. Actually, any artist knows the creative process goes far deeper and no idea is totally original. If one is locked into three dimensional time, one will think he is making up ideas rather than channeling a stream of consciousness.

As will be discussed in other parts of this book, most of us are to some degree locked into three dimensional time by programmed thought (if you weren't, you wouldn't be sitting there reading this book). And, to go straight to the source of it all, who programs such thoughts? The quickest and fastest answer to this question is the Illuminati. They are the world famous conspiratorial group who are deemed to hold the marionette strings to the entire consciousness of Earth and the universe. Their symbol, the eye in the pyramid, appears on the dollar bill. Actually, they are more known for their political and economical conspiracies than for their programming operation or their manipulation of time. (Manipulating time is the key to their entire facade, and keep in mind that possible changes in time could have obscured Thorn E.M.I.'s connection to any parts of this story).

And, who is deeply associated with and sometimes thought to control the Illuminati? None other than Aleister Crowley! This relationship is discussed in depth in the book *Masks of the Illuminati* by Robert Anton Wilson (notice the synchronicity of his surname).

Whatever the case is with Doug Curtis and Mike Janover, there is still a mystery here which only seems to be breeding. No matter how many denials come out in the future about this movie and its sources, it will likely raise more and more questions.

MONTAUK POINT LIGHTHOUSE

Commissioned by President George Washington,
the Montauk Lighthouse is a popular tourist attraction. It is
only a long walk away from the former Montauk Air Force Base.

5

THE CAMERON CLAN

Before I had met Preston, I was well aware of Aleister Crowley and had read some of his scholarly works. I thought it was fascinating that he could possibly be a part of Montauk and that he might be related to some of the major players.

While I was disappointed in my search to find any mention of the Wilson brothers in Crowley's books, I did find reference to a Duncan Cameron in his autobiography *The Confessions of Aleister Crowley*. The full name is actually L.C.R. Duncombe Jewell, but Crowley referred to the man as "Duncan" and said that he was quite proud to claim the name of Cameron. This Duncan Cameron was eager for a Celtic revival and wanted to unite the five Celtic nations in an empire.

The discovery of the name "Duncan Cameron" in Crowley's work was surprising, but more importantly, it led to a data trail which revealed an amazing synchronicity between the Cameron and Crowley families.

I continued to search out some of Crowley's harder to find books and hope that I could find a Wilson mentioned. I was surprised again when I discovered the name "Cameron" also appears in the preface of his book, *The World's*

Tragedy. Crowley is describing a scene from his childhood and he mentions a Mr. and Mrs. Cameron. They were part of his father's fundamentalist Christian sect. Other than a bizarré argument, not much is said about them.

As I poked around in more books by or about Crowley, I discovered that his actual birth name was "Edward Alexander Crowley". He had adopted the name "Aleister". This was interesting to me because Duncan Cameron's first name is "Alexander" as was his father's. "Edward", is of course, the name of Duncan's brother who is now known as Al Bielek. There was also an uncle in the family who was named Edward. He is a bit of a curiosity as he was extremely wealthy from a family business but philandered and drank until he ended up as a homeless person.

These coincidences between the Crowleys and the Camerons were not conclusive of anything in themselves, but all of this was a definite curiosity. Next, I happened to be speaking to a friend of mine by the name of Chelsea Flor and told her about the name associations I'd been finding. I knew she was somewhat familiar with Crowley's materials. She didn't have any further knowledge about Camerons or Wilsons in the Crowley family tree, but she did report an oddity. She said that her sister used to date a man by the name of Cameron Duncan. He had a twin brother and his father was an associate at Princeton University (the same place where the theories for the Philadelphia Experiment were hatched). Cameron Duncan had a strong interest in Crowley and was believed to have experimented heavily with LSD (a mind control drug). The fact that he was a twin was also curious because according to information I'd learned at a Psychotronic meeting, twins were the best candidates for psychic (including psycho-sexual) experimentation in certain secret projects. The Third Reich had also done extensive experimentation with twins.

I asked Chelsea to ask her sister for Cameron Duncan's address and to find out his twin brother's first name. She couldn't come up with the address as it went back too many years, but she did find out that the brother's name was Kimberly.

When I next saw Duncan, I recounted the entire story about Cameron Duncan and he smiled in amusement. He also informed me that this type of phenomena was not so unusual in his life. Doubles for him have been sighted in Los Angeles, a local diner on Long Island and in Plattsburg, New York. When I told his half-brother (Al Bielek) the story, Al simply said, "How many of these guys are there walking around?" None of this was new to him either.

A yet more amazing aspect of this story is that I saved the best for last. I asked Duncan if he had anybody in his family by the name of Kimberly. The answer was yes — his sister!

I continued to find remarkable synchronicity with Duncan's family name. I had met a lady by the name of Claudia Reilly who worked at the Starbrite Book Store on Long Island. While the book was being written, I had told her a little bit about it. She was very interested because she had an unusual experience at Montauk when the project was active. She was a leader of a Girl Scout troop and had seen a UFO there while transporting girl scouts. Although it has not been addressed therapeutically, she experienced missing time and thought it to be an abduction.

Upon reading *The Montauk Project*, she said that she had always known someone in her life who had known a Duncan Cameron. The name had figured in her life in many different respects. It would be seen in store windows, street signs and what not.

Claudia later introduced me to Joy, a psychic friend of hers. Joy has been accurate in telling me things about my personal life. I believe her to be very good in this regard and largely undiscovered as an effective psychic. In another bizarre twist, Joy revealed that she'd been channelling the name "Duncan Cameron" for a year and a half and she had no idea what it meant. She had also gotten the name "Wilson" along with it. In a surprise to her, I was now able to explain some of the significance behind what she had been channeling.

Joy also did a reading which indicated the Wilson brothers were twins (this was not the first time I'd heard this!) and were separated early in life. They were finally reunited in Geneva, Switzerland. She said there was another name associated with them that was something like "Shell", but she couldn't quite get a clear picture. I suggested "Shelley" because I associated Geneva with Percy and Mary Shelley, both famous writers. Joy said, "That's it! Shelley".

I then proceeded to go to the library and research Shelley. I went straight to the biographies without consulting the card catalogue. There was a big thick book about Percy Shelley so I picked it up. The author's last name was Cameron! I was dumbstruck. I would soon find out that his full name was Kenneth Cameron, and he is considered the quintessential scholar on Shelley. Unfortunately, this book didn't provide much information for my investigation, but it did indicate that the Shelley's lived in the same time period as the Wilson brothers supposedly did. The investigation of the Shelleys would lead off in another direction which I've included in Appendix C for those who are interested. I didn't include it in the main text as it hasn't come full circle yet. Whatever the case, the name Cameron was still lurking on the horizon. I was soon to get an even bigger surprise.

These are not the only instances of synchronicity I

experienced with the name "Cameron", but they are some of the more pertinent ones. The most interesting one started in August of 1991 when I had seen a book advertised in a catalogue. It was called *The Collected Essays of John Whiteside Parsons* and was edited by his wife Cameron. I was aware of who Jack Parsons was. He is mentioned in the prelude of this book and had not only been an integral part of the rocket research at Cal Tech but was a student of Aleister Crowley as well. In 1941, he joined the Ordo Templi Orientis* or O.T.O. He would later befriend and engage in magical experiments with L. Ron Hubbard, the founder of Dianetics and Scientology.

I was very surprised to see that Parsons' wife's name was Cameron. There was no first name or anything listed in the catalog. I eventually saw the book in a book store and bought it in May 1992. I read the introduction and back matter of the book to find some more information about Cameron whose first name is Marjorie. The book said that she had served in the Navy in Washington D.C. and joined Parsons after her discharge. I thought that this was all very interesting and I addressed a letter to Hymenaeus Beta. This is the titular name for the person who is the Outer Head of the O.T.O. I asked if he could obtain Cameron's address for me. I was going to write her and hopefully fly out and visit her. I placed the letter in the mail box and proceeded to fly to Los Angeles that very same day for an entirely different purpose. I was going to announce the release of *The Montauk Project* to the American Booksellers Association in Anaheim. This was the location chosen for the 1992 book fair.

---

* Translated, this means Order of the Oriental Templars or Order of the Temple of the East. It is a brotherhood that is "dedicated to the high purpose of securing the Liberty of the Individual and his or her advancement in Light, Wisdom, Understanding, Knowledge, and Power."

I soon noticed a booth that sold Crowley's books. I asked a gentleman there if he had ever heard of Cameron and if he knew where I could obtain her address. He was very direct and referred me to another man who just happened to be in Southern California that very week. I got hold of this man and arranged a meeting with him. We had a long talk. I gave him a copy of *The Montauk Project* so that he could read it and understand what my purpose was. He informed me that Cameron did live in Southern California but that she didn't ordinarily see people. As we continued to talk, it became apparent to me that he was indeed the Outer Head of the O.T.O., the very man I had written a letter to just days earlier. My letter had been addressed to the O.T.O.'s post office box in New York, and I arrived ahead of it in Los Angeles! He requested that I keep his identity secret which I will continue to honor.

After a few days, Cameron agreed to see me. I was given her phone number in order to set up an appointment and was surprised to see that her phone number prominently contained the numbers "666". This was, of course, Aleister Crowley's code. I knew I was on the right track, and it was very exciting.

I won't give away the location of her house, but it created an impression on me that I will never forget. There was a modest but striking entrance that consisted of a high bamboo fence and a sitting Buddha. It was like entering a shrine or holy place. Beyond the entrance one was immediately greeted by the sounds of a bird that sat in a tree. It was an extremely penetrating sound.

A dog at her porch stood guard. Cameron spoke to the dog, and he allowed me to enter. Her house was old with trappings that might be associated with occult. She was in her 70's and possesed a striking presence. An aura of immense knowledge seems to surround her. Cameron speaks with a very strong volition and her words manifest a mastery of occult principles.

We talked for four hours and her stories were quite fascinating. She talked about the old days with her husband Jack, Ron Hubbard and Robert Heinlein. She explained that Heinlein's most famous work *Stranger In A Strange Land* was based upon Crowley's *Book of the Law*. Although Hubbard had crossed her husband and his ventures had financially wiped Jack out, she said that she liked Ron. He and Jack had a complex relationship that was not unlike two brothers. In later life, Hubbard claimed that he had infiltrated Parson's group on behalf of the Government in order to break it up. Church of Scientology officials have claimed this from time to time but the general press have been quick to refute it. Cameron said it wouldn't have surprised her if Hubbard had been a spy as he came from Naval Intelligence. She had also worked for the Navy and said that she had considered the possibility that she had been sent to Parsons on a similar basis. Whatever the case, it seems that someone in the military was very interested in Jack Parsons.

Cameron said she used the name "Cameron" simply because that was her last name and that was what she was called in the Navy. She wanted to make it stick. She was also interested that I had such a strong desire to find out about her family name. The Cameron clan was very important to her family legacy. Her father had told her that before she passes on, she should go to Scotland and be surrounded by Camerons. It would be an essential experience for her.

Cameron also mentioned that she had worked for the Joint Chiefs of Staff and had a very important position of influence. She met Churchill and all the heads of state that visited the country. The head of the Scottish military requested a special audience with her when he heard that her name was Cameron.

Somewhat to my surprise, she had not heard of the Philadelphia Experiment. The Montauk data was new to her as well. I proceeded to give her a quick synopsis of the entire story and synchronistic circumstances between the Crowley and Cameron families.

When I finally finished my story, I began to feel a bit uneasy. What if she had nothing to add? I had already sacrificed an entire day at the book fair and had risked making a nuisance of myself during the entire quest. Was this a dead end?

Strangely, I felt there was no place in the entire universe that I would rather be than sitting there and talking in her kitchen. I felt strongly that she held some key that would unlock the mystery I was pursuing. It also occurred to me that whatever she might say would be totally unexpected. I told her exactly how I felt and waited for her reply. Hopefully, I would not be disappointed.

Cameron was silent for a short while. My whole being was riveted on whatever she was about to say. Finally, she said that it was interesting that I had mentioned the name "Wilson" (when referring to the Wilson brothers) because her actual name wasn't Marjorie Cameron. It was Marjorie Wilson. She was a Wilson! And so was L. Ron Hubbard. His name was Wilson, too!

I was too shocked to respond.

ALEXANDER DUNCAN CAMERON, JR.

Does this man look familiar to you?
He is Duncan Cameron, born on June 29, 1951 and had
extensive psychic training by secretive agencies.
He manned the Montauk Chair during the Montauk experiments
and also remembers travelling between 1943 and 1983
during the Philadelphia Experiment.

ALFRED BIELEK

Al is Duncan's half-brother
and was previously known as Edward Cameron.
He remembers being aboard the *USS Eldridge* with Duncan
during the Philadelphia Experiment, jumping
overboard and landing at Montauk Point.

ALEXANDER DUNCAN CAMERON, SR.

Also known as Duncan Arnold,
he fathered Duncan and Edward Cameron.
Duncan Sr. is a curious engima because of his mysterious connections
with the intelligence community. He spent a lot of time
building sailboats and travelling to Europe and is believed to have
smuggled German scientists into the U.S.

PRESTON B. NICHOLS

Scientist and author, Preston was recognized by many
employees from the Montauk Project before he
investigated it himself and broke the story.
He continues to investigate the phenomena of Montauk
and also maintains his own electronics business.

6

THE WILSON CLAN

Cameron said that her father's original name was Hill Lesley Wilson. He became known as Hill Lesley Cameron because he was adopted by an uncle whose name was Alexander Cameron. Unfortunately, she couldn't remember his middle name.

She explained that the Wilson clan was a subdivision of the Cameron clan. Cameron also said that the Camerons had descended from the Gunn clan, the oldest clan in Scotland. The Gunns came from the Odins who had come over during the Viking period. This perhaps explains why the Camerons were known as the "fiercest of the fighting clans". It also reveals that they have a definite Aryan root.

I was surprised to consider that Hubbard could be a Wilson. Oddly, Cameron has a striking resemblance to Hubbard. And it's not just the fact that they both had flaming red hair. There is a facial resemblance. I asked her how she knew about Hubbard being a Wilson, but she wasn't sure. She remembered reading it somewhere. I checked this out and discovered a reference in a book entitled *Bare Faced Messiah* which said that Hubbard's father Harry Ross Hubbard was really a Wilson and that he had been adopted by a family named Hubbard. I also discovered that Harry Ross Hubbard was born in Iowa within a hundred miles of the birth place of Cameron. It is also ironic to note that Duncan did a reading (before any of this experience of mine) which said that he had some sort of connection to Iowa.

I would later return to the Outer Head of the O.T.O. and tell him about the resemblance between Cameron and Hubbard. He just laughed and said they both came from the same batch!

All this was extremely fascinating, but it left me perplexed as to what it all meant. In one respect, my quest had come full circle. This entire experience validated Preston's memory about the Wilson brothers. It may not have proven it on a court of law basis but even the most dense would observe a synchronicity that is beyond ordinary belief. The Wilsons, Camerons and Crowleys were inextricably connected by some workings which could best be described as magical.

I believe the entire experience can be best explained by what happened next (which I only realized during the writing of this chapter).

Cameron showed me a copy of a quote by José Arguelles, the author of *The Mayan Factor*. It indicated that after July 27, 1992 synchronicity would step up and play a much bigger role in all of our lives. It would continue to increase and is a sign of the times we are living in.

I said good-bye to Cameron and went immediately to a phone booth to call the Arcuri family. These are old family friends who I grew up next door to and hadn't seen in sixteen years. I got on the highway and drove straight for my old neighborhood where I'd lived almost thirty years earlier. I was totally amazed that I was able to drive exactly to my old street without any directions or getting lost. I'd moved from the area when I was ten and had never driven in Southern California prior to this trip.

I was expecting to see huge trees as it had been thirty years since I had lived in the neighborhood. It was astounding to me that all the trees that had grown over the years on the parking strips had been removed and little ones had been replanted. It looked just like it did when I had resided there. It was the same magical place of my childhood and it had an extremely pleasant and stunning time warp effect.

Not only was I coming home to my old neighborhood, the entire experience with Cameron was a homecoming, too. My Scientology experiences had come full circle in a sense and I was also getting to the bottom of a very deep Montauk connection.

It then became obvious to me what the whole importance is behind the entire Montauk story. It is the harbinger of a grand homecoming. We have the opportunity to come home and regain our inheritance. Our consciousness was ripped asunder eons ago. Analogies about this can be read in the Holy Bible and sacred texts from many other sources. The Age of Aquarius has mandated that we will recover the lost knowledge of millennia. Hence, the holocausts of the past are coming to view and we can regain our birthright as fully conscious spiritual beings. But, the work is not yet done. We have to pull back the Wizard's curtain like Toto did in the *Wizard of Oz*. And at this stage, the Wilson brothers would seem to be at least two of the wizards behind the curtain.

According to psychic readings and memories, Preston and Duncan would be incarnations of the Wilson brothers. And while they are wizards in their own right, they are certainly not capable of having all the answers in their present state. It would therefore seem that the Wilson brothers are lost parts of their entire soul bodies, existing in other dimensions and occasionally leaking through (perhaps quite purposely) to the third dimension. And, on a broad level, we all probably have our own "Wilson brother" parts that exist in other dimensions of existence. We will come into contact with these other dimensional soul-parts of ourselves as we fully integrate with the entire universe.

Although the above is philosophical and is probably fairly accurate, we have to continue to pull back the Wizard's curtain in the physical realm. Accordingly, I stumbled upon a rare book in New York City. It was entitled *The Secrets of Aleister Crowley* by Amado Crowley. My first reaction to this book was that it was by a crank. I hadn't heard of Crowley having any sons. But when I looked through it, I was surprised to see a man named "Wilson" mentioned in the book. I bought it and read it. Unfortunately, there was no information about the Wilson brothers, but I found the book quite interesting in that it portrayed a side of Crowley that I'd always suspected but was never quite seen in print. On a deep and subjective basis, I thought the book to be accurate but it is not my position to pass judgment on the legitimate genealogy of the Crowley family. Synchronicity was definitely at play and that is most important.

I wrote to Amado Crowley via the publisher and asked him about the Wilson brothers and if he'd heard of them or if they were related to the Wilson mentioned in his book. It took several months for him to receive the letter. Finally, after all hope of hearing from him had vanished (there were more postal delays en route to me), I received Mr. Crowley's reply.

He said that the Wilson he'd referred to in the book was not a member of the same Wilson family, but he did know of the Wilson brothers. They had actually existed!

According to Amado Crowley, the Wilson brothers were intimate with Aleister and with Grandfather Crowley (Edward Alexander). They were also on close terms with the writer, H.G. Wells, who may have been influenced by them when he wrote his novels about time.

Interestingly, he also mentioned that he understood that the twin brothers were physically sterile. This would at first seem to indicate a dead end as there would be no descendants from which to obtain information about them. However, it does provide a further clue for those who are familiar with the principles of magick. First, it will be necessary to explain some of these principles and relate other stories about Montauk before we can try to solve the mystery of the Wilson brothers.

7

MAGICK AND PSYCHOTRONICS

Now that we have completed our journey into the occult, it is important to give a brief understanding of how magick relates to psychotronics and the work that was done at Montauk. The study of the occult is essential to understanding what happened there.

Crowley defined Magick as "the Science and Art of causing Change to occur in conformity with Will." Magick is parallel to science in that both recognize that natural events follow one another invariably without the intervention of supernatural causes. The entire order and uniformity of nature underlie both systems.

For example, if one wants to use Magick to gain a fortune, one would study the nature of fortunes and the natural laws concerning such. The practitioner would then align himself in proximity with these forces and accordingly be the recipient of such. It goes without saying that one should of course study himself in detail and be sure that it is indeed one's natural course to obtain a fortune. If not, one could be scorched or suffer accordingly in regard to the principles of nature. Hence, stealing would not be without its consequences.

Magick departs from conventional science at a very key point. Science understandably measures the universe in terms of quantity. When a scientist can't measure something, he won't consider it because it has no basis for existence according to his system. His investigation will pursue no further. Magick, on the other hand, continues on from that point. It is definitely a rarefied art form in its higher levels. Magick is said to be scientific at that level but it is hard to communicate the principles in terms of ordinary language and common Earth experience. Accordingly, it becomes an esoteric subject and is usually mastered only by initiates.

We can build a bridge from conventional science to Magick when we realize that we live in a multi-dimensional universe(s). If this concept cannot be grasped empirically or through direct experience, it can be arrived at by logical progression. For example, if there are three dimensions, it stands to reason there would be at least a fourth. Traveling around on a piece of paper and talking to two dimensional beings might be frustrating. They would likely think you are crazy talking about a third dimension. There would be no way they could experience it without rising to the third. This is a similar analogy to our world and the fourth dimension. The higher realm cannot be isolated simply by using the tools of the lower dimension.

Although scientists routinely use mathematics to measure the universe, they do not seem preoccupied with the fact that mathematical principles are entirely absolute and have no existence in this three dimensional universe. That very "absolute universe" of mathematics is integral to our survival in today's world. Therefore, we can give credence to other universes besides our physical world. As science ordinarily only measures in terms of three dimensions, it becomes necessary to go beyond that. This is what the study of the occult is actually all about: going beyond the realms of ordinary experience.

It is intriguing to one's own personal being that one could conceivably take a being from the fourth dimension (or an even higher state) and make them think they could only respond to ideas of a three dimensional nature. This is simply programmed thought and is the exact antithesis (opposite) of creativity.

All of this makes it abundantly clear that it is the God-like and angelic (both creative) forces that take us to the higher dimensions and that is the satanic and demonic forces that approach the lower domains. It is theologically satanic to argue on behalf of three dimensions only.

Magick properly concerns itself with quantity, just as regular science does, but it also embraces quality, which could be considered the quality or character of life itself in all its myriad manifestations.

In the Philadelphia Experiment, it was the human factor that suffered. Humans were thrown out of this dimension and their references to ordinary reality suffered accordingly. The human factor equates to the character and quality of life. All of these weird and secretive experiments have run amok because they have not accounted for the human factor. All of this brings us to a very good question. What is the character and quality of life itself?

The answer to that question would seem to be in the question itself. Life is character and quality. Human beings have a particular nature and character that are not quantifiable. It is this dichotomy which results in technological nightmares where you find Science versus Man.

The closest bridge between science and spiritual beings could be observed in the field of psychotronics.

There, man can be measured to some degree. His individuality can be recognized by specific frequencies and wave lengths. Such frequencies would not necessarily be the individual for absolute purposes but would be the manifestation of the individual for practical or technological purposes.

With psychotronics, one can tune in to a specific frequency and snare it, thereby also snaring the individual. It is done by isolating the specific frequency and wave length and jamming it or otherwise perturbing its freedom of motion. This would make the individual (as actually observed by the change in frequencies, etc.) change his signature or basic characteristics. He would have to change them if he didn't want to be continually bombarded by the jamming frequency. This means that the person would be changing himself and therefore would no longer be himself. If he was further induced into adopting frequencies that were controllable or suggestible, he could easily become a controlled person.

All of this can be easily brought to mind if you imagine a petite ballerina who is floating across a room in sacred dance. She is being her natural self. If she is bombarded by aggressive and coarse wave lengths (which can be found in certain coarse noises), she would stop dancing and cover her ears. Her dance would become impossible. She would become obsessed with covering her ears so as not to hear the noise. Finally, she would become deaf and degraded to a point where she wouldn't want to think about dancing. Dancing could even become associated with being painful. A woman who had been indoctrinated in such a fashion would probably jump at the opportunity to become a mundane middle class housewife. That's quite a relief compared to being hammered with a "buzz saw". But in this case, it's a far cry from being

or manifesting her true self.

This illustrates how humans can react to electronics with the principles of magick ever lurking in the background. When the order of life is enhanced such magick can be considered white. When the harmony and order of life is reversed, one is dealing with black magic.

Magick is a deep subject and it is not the place of this book to go into it in depth. Those who are interested can study it in different texts.

We will now return to the real life people and unfolding drama concerning the Montauk Project.

8

MISTER X

In an earlier chapter I referred to a Mr. X who claimed he had been involved in the Montauk Project. He'd supposedly managed a huge portfolio that financed the operations and also worked in the area of procurement. According to legend, his work was crucial to obtaining the technology from the aliens for the Montauk chair.

At our meeting, Mr. X said he would not be able to divulge any more information about his own role. He was nervous so we proceeded to talk about other things. I asked him about the photo of Preston with the Wilson brothers which Mr. X had supposedly seen, too. No new information would come forth on this subject, but he had some very interesting things to say about Aleister Crowley and Montauk.

Mr. X said that Crowley was actually manipulating time back in the teens and twenties of this century. He was able to go backwards and forwards in time through a purely magical basis. Further, Crowley was also familiar with principles of levitation and was known to have spirits materialize in both sound and physical form.

One of the reasons Crowley was able to travel in time, Mr. X explained, was that he was not locked to any dimension or illusion. This is not new to the subject of metaphysics and has also been performed by other psychics and trance mediums who actually get into a symbolic state. This would be an altered state of consciousness where they would read information, like the akashic records. There is a level beyond the akashic which deals with entities or energy forces that go into other bodies or go into other dimensions (or existences). Crowley was able to go beyond the set norm and project himself into different planes of existence. Thus, he was not only ahead of his time but was exterior to time itself.

At this point in our conversation, the possibility occurred to me that Crowley was creating worm holes from the physical realm to other realities and back again. Perhaps even the bizarre manipulations at Montauk and in Philadelphia could have been elaborate physical deployments at the behest of simply one very powerful magician. It is highly ironic that The Beast was Crowley's own chosen logo and that this was the materialization that appeared at Montauk. Crowley was notorious for finding ways to get attention and in some ways this book could be considered an elaborate advertisement for his work. That is definitely not the intended purpose, but his connection and synchronicity to the entire project cannot be denied.

Mr. X and I had now reached an understanding and it seemed that he had wanted me to know exactly what Crowley's role was. I also think that it is interesting to note that he spoke about this subject with an authority that is not usual to his normal manner.

He also said that the Catholic Church had a tendency to make a story much grander than it actually was and therefore manipulate people. Crowley was operating on an even higher level. He was bringing in pagan deities and energy forces (sometimes black or negative) that are all part of the collective unconscious (could also be called preconscious or simply imagination). This is the same unconscious where angels and religious visions come from. Crowley went beyond the artificially contrived boundaries of the Church and state and was not in agreement with the machinations which kept the masses ignorant. He dealt with pure magic and knew it on an intuitive level that was both deep and experiential.

Mr. X concluded our discussion by admitting that he was frightened. Crowley had remarkable powers and ability which few others possess. He thought of Crowley as a wild joker who was romping around and having a good time without regard to how it might affect us. I recognized this joker aspect as "The Fool" from the tarot deck. This is the wild creative impulse that started the whole universe. It is a creative force that creates willy-nilly, on whim and without regard to consequences.

After this talk, I searched through books trying to find out if there was any documentation on any of this. Mr. X seemed to be sharing some sort of private data base so I didn't really expect to find any in common literature. I concluded that there might be something to find in 1923. That was twenty years prior to 1943 and coincided with the twenty year biorhythms of the Earth that were explained in the first book. I had a great deal of difficulty finding any reference to 1923 and where Crowley might have been. I eventually gave up the search.

Finally, I arrived at the doorstep of Maria Fix, my psychic friend. Although I'd made an appointment with her, she was surprised at my arrival and asked what I was doing there. She seemed to have her schedule mixed up. We were just supposed to go over various information about Montauk when she suddenly said, "I know why you're here!".

She whisked me away in her car to a friend of hers who had a whole case of books, most of them by Aleister Crowley. Some of them were rare books that I'd never seen before. Upon taking them home and scouring through them, I found a book entitled *The Magical Diaries of Aleister Crowley*. This book contained a diary for one year only: 1923!

I immediately looked for the entry for August 12th, the day the Philadelphia Experiment took place. This date and the 13th were missing. Almost every other day had an entry. Reading the diary indicates he may have been sick during these days. Someone else suggested these entries were purposefully omitted. Whatever the case, it was extremely rare for Crowley to omit writing in his magical diary on any particular day.

As a side note, Crowley also mentions in these diaries that he picked up an odd colony of blisters while at Montauk and they stayed with him for at least five years. No further mention is made of Montauk in this book.

None of this research through his diaries properly documents Crowley being involved directly with the Montauk project. It only leaves us with another odd instance of synchronicity. I did, however, find something of interest in another book.

In the book, *Eight Lectures on Yoga*, Crowley makes it very clear that he understood the subtleties of electro-magnetism and how it interfaced with gravity. He was far beyond the mundane scientists of his day (and ours, too). He also is on record for stating that space is "finite yet boundless" and was amused that Einstein would shake the world four years after his own public statement by detailing the very same point with mathematical formulas. Crowley's understandings were not just from his own brilliance. He had been schooled in sacred geometry and many other alchemical disciplines from ancient orders. The scientific crowd that heralded Einstein toed the line of the establishment and were coming from an entirely different quarter.

It has long been said that science can only hope to arrive at what religion has known for millennia. Crowley, being steeped in all sorts of religion and mythology, would seem to be a prime example of that old saw. He was ahead of everyone.

None of this information should be considered as a glorification of Aleister Crowley. He lived as a human and died as a human. If we believe the information trail he left, he had very severe shortcomings as a human being. His scholarship was brilliant beyond belief. In this book, I have attempted to relay some of the best aspects of the man as they seem to be the most important. They also tie into the story.

Before we embark on the next part of the book and read Preston's entries, it is important to note one other thing that Crowley pointed out in *Eight Lectures on Yoga*. He lectured to an audience that science is a closed system because it does not assign human values to its descriptions of the universe. If values form an integral part of reality, it seems strange that science gives a consistent description of phenomena which ignores them.

This brings us right back once again to the human factor that was abused during the Philadelphia Experiment and Montauk Project. This is the most important factor in the universe.

TOWN OF MONTAUK

A view looking east on Montauk Highway about seven miles from
Camp Hero (the old Montauk Air Force Base).
The main strip of Montauk is only about a quarter mile long.
The town branches out in different directions
with many hills and gulleys.

PART
II

BY PRESTON B. NICHOLS

II

INTRODUCTION
TO PART II

I have been investigating and talking about the Montauk story for over a decade, and while it is not my intention to convince anyone of anything, there are important developments that have occurred that I believe are in the public interest to know about. You should make up your own mind as to their relative truth and what should be done about the information presented.

What will be relayed in this section of the book are events that I have experienced since the writing of *The Montauk Project*. These will reveal a larger scenario to Montauk than just myself and Duncan.

I am particularly concerned about the group we refer to as the Montauk boys. For those who do not remember, the Montauk boys were those who were programmed with psychosexual mind control techniques. The following information concerning them was initially arrived at by interviews with various people who had been part of the project. Duncan's readings also played a big part in figuring out what was going on. A major breakthrough with the psychic investigation of this project came when I came into contact with a man who had supposedly programmed the boys. He was sent to prison after he began to work with me and his real name has been witheld to protect him and his family. I will refer to him as Stan Campbell in this book. Without his cooperation, it would have been extremely difficult for me to have acquired all of the following information concerning the Montauk boys.

First, I will give an overall description of the Montauk boys project and follow that with the bizarre events I experienced with Stan. Finally, I will go into another strange encounter which led to an investigation of the history of the electronic transistor and alien involvement in such. As the story flows, it all strongly points to the Montauk Project being active today.

9

THE MONTAUK BOYS

Back in the early 1970's, the Montauk group became interested in programming children. According to legend, gray aliens picked up about fifty kids and delivered them to Montauk. They would then be programmed and separated into three groups: ages 6-12, 13-16, and 16-22.

The first group, after they were processed, and if they survived the processing, were placed into two separate subgroups. One would go to the grays for genetic experimentation. The other subgroup would be programmed and put back into society. Sometimes they would return to their original family; other times they would be inserted into a new family.

The idea with these younger children was to have them assimilate into the population. They would be groomed to be normal pillars of society and would go to college and become lawyers, doctors, politicians or whatever. These people are sleepers in the sense that when the secret government wants to activate them, they will be on call. They could be answerable on both a psychotronic/ hypnotic basis or verbal command. The plan is to activate them when chaotic times come so that they band together into vigilante squads and go after government enemies.

Their instructions are not specific other than to go after anyone believed to be anti-government and to commit general destruction against anti-government groupings.

The second two groups, ages 13-16 and 17-22, were also used for genetic material and for infiltration into society, but their programming was for more immediate results. Again, those programmed were placed into two subgroups, if they survived the programming. The first were a hit squad of mindless assassins. These particular agents could be set up and triggered to go after one particular person. The second subgroup was called "The Disrupters" and they were the spearheads for the satanic movement and similar style cults. Their job was to organize and subvert on an immediate basis as opposed to the younger kids who were long range sleepers. In some cases, the older youths, ages 17-22 were also groomed to be slave workers.

The programming of all these youths started in 1973, but there have been suggestions that it was going on at Brookhaven (Brookhaven National Laboratories on Long Island) much earlier. The reason they looked for blue eyed blonds has to do with a psychic genetic factor believed to reside in the Aryan race. This is an ancient occult doctrine that has to do with the different root races on planet Earth and is parallel to the interests of Hitler and his researchers. There were also some with darker hair and skin but most fit the Aryan look.

The programmers concentrated on three particular ages: 9, 14 and 19. Each of these was considered a peak age. They would put the kids in a room stark naked. Radio sensitive electronic paraphernalia was placed on their genitalia and a diabolic program was started where they would be treated brutally, not unlike a Pavlovian dog. These kids would be beaten to within inches of their lives until they were mentally broken, consciousless hulks. Many died. Those that were able to survive it became extremely suggestible in the extreme.

While the kids were being broken, rod like antenna structures were placed in the room. I believe this was an alien device that was designed to pick up the patterns of fear and hopelessness. Someone was apparently recording these patterns. The boys that died were analyzed and had certain body parts removed. These body parts were significant because of the state they were in when the boys died at the height of fear. UFO folklore has it that the gray nation is very interested in our fear. It has been suggested that they harvest our fright. At Montauk, it is possible that this kids scenario was originally set up by the grays for their own purposes. It is also possible that they suggested it and the Montauk brass did it for their own purposes.

Once the kids were broken, they were sent to a programmer who would then rebuild their minds in the way that those in charge wanted them rebuilt. The entire subconscious would be reconstructed from the ground up. The minds were always programmed for a particular purpose. Then, they would be let loose on the world.

MONTAUK MYSTERY CLOSETS

Around the neighborhood of the Montauk base there are different
small structures with doors, such as the one above.
They sometimes are equipped with red lights which might be part
of an alarm system. Some have speculated that they could be entrances
to the underground, but we are not absolutely sure.
The structures are a mystery.

10

STAN CAMPBELL, CIA APPLICANT

In 1991, I was asked to appear at a lecture in the New York metropolitan area. I was invited by Elaine Donald, a practicing psychic who was the hostess for the evening. After the lecture was over, she asked if I could give a ride home to one of her students. His name was Stan Campbell (fictitious name). Based upon what I now know, this entire meeting could have been a setup.

Stan was quiet during the lecture but wanted to discuss things afterwards. I told him to save it for the ride home. There, he let loose, describing problems as an abductee, problems with the Government and consequent legal difficulties. He had been accused of embezzlement but didn't remember doing it. Although he recalled opening bank accounts and getting money from somewhere, he wasn't sure exactly what he'd done. Generally, he talked of all his life problems. Before we got to his house, he said he'd like to work with me. I eventually let him off and agreed to see him at a future date.

As I began to work with Stan, I found him very cooperative. In fact, he was suspiciously cooperative. I observed that his mind was almost total mush. He would unquestioningly do anything that was asked of him. There was no doubt in my mind that somebody had seriously violated this man. I heard all sorts of stories about him going to different UFO groups. He also told me about seeing a psychiatrist and a particular bad experience at an encounter group which had been conducted like an inquisition.

I took most of what he said at less than face value. He was paranoid, his mind was weak and he virtually had no will of his own. He was very hard to work with so I suggested we use some of Wilhelm Reich's methods. (These are methods of accessing a person's subconscious which are much deeper than ordinary hypnosis. They were used at Montauk and by other secret mind control operations.) He said fine. The first thing I noticed was that he responded to them as if he'd been trained with them. For him to respond the way he did, I would normally have had to work with him for a couple of months to get him to that level. This told me right away that he'd had experience with these techniques. Although he claimed he couldn't remember, I am sure that he was trained in the Wilhelm Reich methods.

As we worked, Stan began to come up with UFO abduction experiences. In a nutshell, he had apparently been abducted by various alien groups. He also had recollections of abductions by human types (allegedly government personnel) in UFOs.

Eventually, Stan started to remember activity with the CIA. In the early 1980's, he had received a phone call at 3:00 A.M. with someone requesting that he apply for work at the CIA. He was told to report to a specific place and fill out application forms. Subsequently, he was requested to go to the New York Institute of Technology and take a test. He was contacted again and told that he did extremely well on the test. Then, he was told to report to a particular hotel (I recall it being The New Yorker) under an assumed name and that there would be a room waiting for him. He gave a false name, was given a key and went in and waited. Stan said the room was suspicious because it was next to a utility closet and there was a mirror on the wall next to the closet. He was fairly sure that there were cameras and surveillance equipment behind the mirror. After a while, the phone rang and a lady came up and gave him a battery of psychological tests.

He returned home and was eventually contacted again. He was told that he'd done very well on the tests and that he had to report to the final testing section. This unit was in Virginia in a town I remember being called Crabwell Corners. There, he went to a Holiday Inn. He was sure it wasn't open to the public because it always had "no vacancy" signs yet there were never people in it. Each room had car keys and other things that went along with it. Stan was given another fictitious name and told to go to a room on the second floor and wait. A number of people came in and did more tests. During the tests, he was sent from one room to another. The whole experience was very strange and he didn't remember half of it.

The "testing" was odd, to say the least. He remembered waking up stark naked with his rear end up in the air. A lot of times different parts of his body would hurt. Three out of the four days he was there, his anal opening hurt. This was about all he remembered. He was eventually told that the testing was complete and that he should go home and wait for further instructions.

After two or three weeks, Stan grew impatient and called a number that had been given him. He was told that he wasn't needed at this time, but the agency would keep everything on file.

All of the above was his conscious recollection. His wife has also indicated that he was involved with an application for the CIA, but I'm not sure if all of this was some sort of a hoax and she was in on it with him.

In my opinion, the only proof of any of this is what he remembered under the Reich method. In certain trance states, unless you're heavily trained, it's almost impossible to lie. These states I am referring to would be much deeper than general hypnosis and lying under them would be similar to lying under truth serum (sodium penathol or the like).

While in such a trance state, Stan went back to the time he applied for the CIA at the New York Institute of Technology. He recalled nothing unusual there or at the hotel he had stayed in during that trip. But when he got down to the hotel in Virginia, he recalled an incident where two guys came to his room at 10:00 A.M. They told him to get undressed and rolled him up in a rug on the floor. He was then put in a stretch limo trunk, driven to a wooded area, taken out of the rug and told to sit in the back seat of the car. From there, the two guys drove him to an old castle estate. There was a big entrance room with a man in the middle who registered them. They went over and pushed a button on the wall. It opened and Stan was popped into an elevator. After descending down what was thought to be two or three levels, the elevator doors opened to a room about twenty feet square.

In the center of the room was a table with a foam cushion on it. The top was hollowed out for a human form. There were actually two cushions so that one could lie face up or face down. Stan was put on his back. Then, a device came down and inserted something into his navel. It hurt like hell as there was no anesthetic.

At this point, he started to recollect shock "therapy".

Different programs were recalled. One was to go into a major corporation whereupon he'd be hired on the spot as a financial officer. The corporation would be expecting him. There, he'd misdirect funds outside the corporation for Project MALTA, which signifies "Montauk Alsace-Lorraine Time Archives". He was diverting funds for the carry on of the Montauk Project in Europe which is situated in the Alsace-Lorraine mountains.

Before Stan left, another panel opened up and there was a gray alien who ducked as if he didn't want to be seen. Maybe he did want to be seen. No one is quite sure. Whatever that was about, someone decided that they had to get him back to his room at the Holiday Inn by 4:00 P.M., and they did just that. Apparently, something else was happening at that time.

It was at this point that Stan's recollection stopped. He couldn't go any further as it was too upsetting.

..."the powers at Montauk were trying to usurp the very power of God."

✝

11

THE DEVIL'S CHAPTER

When Stan told me he was involved with Montauk, I was not surprised. In fact, I had suspected that he'd been at the base at some point. On different occasions, he reported waking up and seeing a man's face in the window. This face stared and laughed at him. This was upsetting to Stan and when he met Duncan he recognized that it was Duncan's face. Meeting Duncan was like a nightmare walking right into reality as a real live person. We concluded that Stan must have been a target from Montauk and that he somehow must have psychically put together the identity of the man (Duncan) who had generated the forms that were bugging him. I would shortly find out that the psychological connection between Stan and Duncan went much deeper.

Eventually, we asked Duncan's information source (this refers to a metaphysical information source) if Stan could come over. Duncan's reading said that Stan was not a security risk. But first, we decided that it would be desirable for Stan to take control of himself because he was evidently under the influence of alien life forms. Actually, he was under the control of quite a few different aliens. We worked fairly fast and feverishly to put Stan in control. Stan was able to channel the aliens directly. He would do a genuine transchannel with the alien entity speaking directly through him. Duncan and a friend named Peter (not Peter Moon) verified that there was something speaking through Stan that was not Stan himself. We eventually got him to the point where he was in control. He could command who and what came in. At that point, Duncan's information source indicated that Stan could come to Space-Time Labs.

As Stan came to Space-Time Labs for the first time, he had emotional troubles as he approached the place. He broke down and cried and started to remember his involvement with the Montauk boys. He said that he was originally picked up by gray aliens in 1973, taken out to Montauk and put through the early Montauk boy program.

It was realized by the Montauk program directors that Stan had some psychic resonance with Duncan, but he was diverted from the program and became a liaison. He became one of the directors in charge of disciplining and breaking the kids. The retrieval of this memory explained for him why he had compulsions at times to be rough with his own kids. He was acting out his life from Montauk. Ordinarily, Stan is one of the most mild mannered people you'd want to meet. But he says his kids will drive him to the point where he becomes like a commandant. He was visibly shaken up by this realization and wanted to undergo a psychic trance to see if what he thought was valid. This was accomplished and approached from many different directions. He kept coming up with the same thing which meant that it had actually happened or that it was a learned response.

What Stan described under trance fit in with what other Montauk boys had described. There was the mention of a five sided room in what appeared to be a damp underground. He described a cage made out of heavy meshed chicken wire (which can be seen out at Montauk today and has been recorded on my video *The Montauk Tour*). He spoke of bodies on tables that were practically in suspended animation, waiting to be programmed or waiting to be sent back after programming. There was also mention of bodies being sent back with big burn holes in the center of the chest and gut. Duncan had spoken about this before but not in the presence of Stan. This was a completely independent account. Now, Stan's information was jiving with Duncan's. There was now no question that they had known each other. Consequently, we delved deeper and deeper.

In what is perhaps the most dramatic and sensational recall that I have ever witnessed, Stan had a recollection of being on the planet Mars and giving something to a robed figure on Mars. He was asked to go back slightly before this incident whereupon he found himself being programmed on a table at Montauk. He was in a chair that had some sort of electroshock setup with a helmet. Stan recalled putting the helmet on and going into an electroshock response that he was now reliving. The next thing he saw was a rectangular opening appearing above the table where they had done the programming. He was sucked right up into the rectangular opening and found himself dressed in early Jewish robes about the time of Christ.

The next thing Stan knows, he's in the time of Christ. His mission, as he remembers it, is to go find Jesus and do two things. First, he's supposed to remove a sample of blood and then he's supposed to kill Him. He finds Christ, and Christ greets him in a most surprising fashion. He says that He knows what Stan is there for and He even volunteers to give him the sample of blood. But, Christ indicates

111

that He is not ready to die yet. He tells Stan that he will not be able to kill Him. Operating on his orders from Montauk, Stan then reports emptying a revolver into Christ without phasing Him.

The whole experience might have lasted for ten hours in terms of Montauk time but Stan felt that he had been in the time of Christ for about two months. We believe that Stan may have somehow become Judas or walked into his body. Somehow it seemed that he assumed the identity of Judas, betrayed Christ and arranged for His death as reported in the Bible. Again, this was all on order from Montauk.

None of this is terribly clear. It is also highly controversial from a religious point of view. I am simply reporting what was recalled and am offering it as raw data. I will add my own conclusions and the reader is invited to do the same.

Stan reported that he brought a vial of blood from Christ back to Montauk. He didn't want to give it up and continued to hold on to it. Then, he felt a burning and the blood "went through him" like an exorcism. He was subsequently sent through a portal to Mars and told to hand over the blood to Christ who he would find on Mars. Stan then emerged out of the underground on Mars and saw a mountain range. Near a mesa, in the corner of a group of rocks, stood a tall thin figure who looked like Christ in robes. He walked over and nervously extended the blood to the robed figure. As the figure accepted the blood, he looked up and Stan now saw the face of Duncan Cameron, masquerading as Christ. Duncan stood there frozen for a number of minutes and Stan took off. The time context of this is not known but we guess that it is late July of 1983 because of some incidents that Duncan has additionally reported on.

Stan then went back to the Martian underground, popped into the vortex and returned to Montauk. There, he was told there that they wanted the blood because it could be mixed into Duncan's bloodstream in such a manner that Duncan would have the same DNA blood coding as that which is on the Shroud of Turin. This could then be used as an argument (quite falsely) that Duncan is the second coming of Christ. Whether the exact details of the incident are accurate, this aspect of the story rings true because Duncan's training (in his current body, born in 1951) had groomed him all along to be the Antichrist.

Stan and Duncan had many similar recollections completely independent of each other which indicated the incredible story I have just told to be true on some level. What is perhaps the most ironic part of all this is that it offers a plausible explanation for why the Montauk Project was crashed. In the first book, I only reported what was known at that time. Somebody had activated a program in Duncan that released Junior (the beast) and frightened everyone into stopping the entire project.

According to what we've been able to put together, Duncan had been trained to be the Antichrist. He can remember the training and is very uncomfortable whenever the subject is brought up. It can even trigger a severe reaction. None of this information is new.

It should also be noted that there are twelve major mystery schools on planet Earth. Each of these secret societies has their own agenda and each is concerned with the fostering of the Antichrist. This is an extremely complex subject loaded with conspiracies. I'm not going to go into it here, but it will be touched on later in the book.

What apparently happened during this ridiculous and perhaps unprecedented manipulation of time is that the powers at Montauk were trying to usurp the very power of

God. Christ, as the representative of God, got the last laugh. His blood was wanted for diabolic purposes, but He reversed the entire process. The blood ended up having a cleansing effect on Duncan and changed his entire personality. Before that incident, Duncan was conceited and arrogant. Afterwards, he became quite a nice person. His first order of business was to meet with a cabal of people at Montauk who would sabotage the project. An arrangement was made to release Junior and the Montauk Project became inoperable. Although it is still active in some form today, the Montauk operatives are not believed to have anywhere near the capability they had in 1983.

The previous story sounds as weird and unusual to me as it probably does to you. It it bothers you too much, please reread Chapter One and try and understand it from the within the context of mythology. It has been reported because it came up in the due course of my research. I did not make it up, and I don't believe Stan did. It also checks out with Duncan's information source. The important point is that it indicates the Christ consciousness prevailed and saved us all from possible manipulation by the Montauk Project. Mankind can be saved from devastation and there are higher forces at work that we can align ourselves with.

Meanwhile, Stan had a serious real life situation to deal with.

12

STAN GOES TO JAIL

I continued to work with Stan after we discovered the strange incidents surrounding Duncan and Mars. Suddenly, his legal problems escalated. He had been accused of embezzlement of funds from the Charles Food Company (fictitious name), a major corporation on Long Island. As the comptroller for this company, he was the key financial officer and had the ability to transfer large sums. His whole legal case was surrounded by strange circumstances. I will give a brief description of these before I continue the story about his legal problems. Some of the information has been contributed by Al Bielek.

The Charles Food Company's connections to Montauk run deep. They are also deeply tied into the mob. Some believe that Charles is a front agency that the secret government uses to handle all sorts of problems. It is believed that the Charles Food trucks used to go all over Long Island and pick up youngsters for the Montauk programming.

When Montauk crashed in 1983, there were plenty of kids from the programming that had to be taken care of. They weren't simply abandoned on a wholesale basis, although we're sure that some were. A financial trust fund was set up to handle the kids but this eventually ran out of money. Stan was then selected to handle this problem, apparently by the CIA. He was indoctrinated, as previously discussed, and sent to the Charles Food Company in about 1985. There, he was ordered to take the job of Comptroller and continue certain clandestine financial arrangements which were already set up. One of these was to withdraw laundered money from Charles and send it to Germany to keep Project MALTA (the continuation of the Phoenix or Montauk Project) going.

Stan was also told to set up a new trust fund for the kids. The money was to be placed in his account by Charles and he would set up the trust. This was a crucial mistake on his part as it made him vulnerable and culpable if anything should go wrong. His masters knew exactly what they were doing. Surprisingly, Stan balked at his orders and became hard to deal with.

Al Bielek remembers hearing of a meeting where Stan was being raked over the coals for not setting up the trust. The money just sat there in his own personal account. He was specifically told that it was his task to set up the fund and that was why he was at the Charles Food Company in the first place. Even though he was allowed a 1 percent management fee for all the monies transferred, he continued to be obstinate. Finally, his masters had enough and he was nailed for misappropriation of funds in 1988. On the advice of his attorney, Stan pleaded guilty to bank fraud. This plea was offered in lieu of being prosecuted for embezzlement of about $400,000.

In a strange twist, the Government had postponed sentencing because Stan had agreed to cooperate with a case against the Charles family for income tax fraud. An "honest" faction of the Government was prosecuting Charles for their own reasons. Stan's defense hoped to show that he didn't commit the embezzlement other than as a stooge for the Charles family. There were allegedly millions of dollars embezzled out of the corporation. The money Stan "took" was from a $400,000 stash which was essentially his cut of it. This means that the entire sum misappropriated would have amounted to some $40,000,000.

During this period, Stan described receiving threatening phone calls and Molotov cocktails were thrown in his driveway. I even remember my mother reading the paper about a house in Stan's town which had one or two Molotovs thrown at it. It actually did happen. The Charles family was probably trying to frighten him and keep him from testifying against them.

In the meantime, the Government got mad and strung out the case. He would be notified months ahead that his sentencing would be on such and such a day. A day or two before the sentencing was to take place, Stan's lawyer would call and say that it had been postponed again. Sentencing would again be in a couple of months. Then, just at the point where he began to remember his involvement in the Montauk Project, he gets a call and is told that he's going to be sentenced that Friday. This was highly unusual because prior to this he'd always had a month or so notice. Now, he was scared.

Stan went to a meeting with his lawyer and claimed that black helicopters had been circling the building. His lawyer was real nasty and told him that the sentencing had been postponed for a couple of days. At this point, I began to threaten over the phone (which I know to be tapped) that if Stan was locked up, I would go and prove the Montauk Project as much as I could and also go public on my involvement in the Moriches Bay UFO crash (I helped to "shoot" it down when I worked for BJM by jamming its drive with the appropriate frequencies—a whole other story). Stan returned to his lawyer's office after we made the threats and was told that the sentencing would be in two weeks. The lawyer was suddenly very nice and "goody-goody".

Next, Stan was hauled into court and the lawyer did a very good job of explaining what had transpired. He said that the prosecuting attorney had not been able to fulfill the Government's part of the deal (as far as getting Stan off the hook for assisting in the tax evasion case against the Charles family). Additionally, the Government said there was nothing further to be pursued. Stan's lawyer wanted a mitigated sentence because two years had lapsed since legal proceedings had commenced.

The judge was sympathetic and said that he personally agreed that the case had been totally mismanaged. Unfortunately, it was out of his hands and he said he had to go by the guidelines given to him. He then asked the prosecuting attorney if he would agree to a lesser sentence by putting this man on probation. The attorney said that under no circumstances should Stan be put on probation. He should be locked up with the maximum sentence. The judge then indicated he had no choice. If he were to rule in favor of probation, the court above him would overturn his ruling and he would get in trouble. The judge then followed his guidelines and took the different points of the case into account. He sentenced Stan to thirty-three months in prison. Parole could be granted after eleven months. He was given thirty days to straighten out his affairs.

I had tried to keep Stan out of prison by making threats over the phone. Judging by the reaction of his attorney, it did seem to carry some weight, but it obviously didn't work out the way I'd hoped. The strategy now became to let things slip and maybe the prosecution would suspend the sentencing. We thought that this plan might be working because he had so many postponements of his sentencing. Stan actually had about three months between sentencing and prison. The federal marshals kept telling him they couldn't find a place to put him. Then, I heard something very interesting through the grapevine. A guy in federal prison camp at Danbury, Connecticut told me that Stan was proposed to go there but they didn't want him because there was too much controversy around him. More delay ensued.

Our next strategy was to try to keep someone from brainwashing him while in prison. It was at this point that John Ford got involved. John is the head of the Long Island UFO Network and was instrumental in the investigation of the Center Moriches UFO crash. John set Stan up for an interview on Geraldo Rivera's "Now It Can Be Told" program and also arranged publicity nationwide. This way, the Government wouldn't dare monkey with Stan.

At about the same time, John quite innocently introduced Stan to a woman who we will refer to as Mary Snodgrass (fictitious name). She was an abductee who turned psychic and had a good reputation working with abductees. John also knew she had excellent connections, but he didn't know for sure what those connections were.

Mary knew exactly how to push Stan's buttons. It was almost as if she had a whole profile on Stan right in front of her. She literally took Stan and totally changed him. This turned him around one hundred eighty degrees. First, she got him to refuse the publicity. Then, she got him to believe that the incidents he remembered were real but were only in his mind. According to this account, Stan was never physically anywhere. Mary maintains a theory that there are no physical abductions but only mental ones. She prepared him for prison and he called her everyday during this period. Mary literally became his "manager" and was talking to Stan more than his own wife.

Finally, Stan Campbell was sentenced to the federal penitentiary in Ashland, Kentucky.

13

STAN IS SILENCED

It is interesting to note that some of this information might not have come to light in this book except for a strange occurrence that happened with Peter Moon. Peter had never met Stan and was skeptical as to whether Stan had any real connection to Montauk at all. He thought the Christ story was interesting and that it had great dramatic and mythological value whether it was "true" in the physical sense or not. Stan's story turned out to be a bit deeper than he expected.

In the autumn of 1992, Al Bielek called Peter Moon and told him that he was coming to Long Island soon. He wanted to know if there might be any speaking engagements available even with extremely short notice. Peter said there wasn't enough time but that he would make a few calls. His first call was to Elaine Donald, the psychic who introduced me to Stan Campbell. He didn't know Elaine but had her business card and knew she organized lectures. She informed Peter that she had too much UFO subject matter lately and that Al wouldn't fit in with her current program. She asked some questions about the Montauk book and wanted to know if he knew Stan Campbell. Peter said he didn't and she said that Stan was a very dear friend. She wanted Peter to visit her in New York because she had some things to tell him that she couldn't say over the phone.

Peter visited her and they generally got to know each other. Then, she wanted to know what he knew about Stan. She was told the Christ story mainly as Peter didn't know the details of Stan's embezzlement. Elaine said that all the things that Stan came up with were under the influence of the drug Prozac and that he wanted nothing to do with Montauk. First, she insisted that his name not be used in the book. Peter readily agreed to this but she went a step further and said that none of the information that Stan came up with should be used either. It was all pure hallucination and/or delusion. She was trying to convince Peter of something.

Next, Elaine said that Peter should call Stan at prison. Stan could then tell him that the Montauk information was all fabrication or delusion, at least as far as it concerned Stan. Peter explained that he didn't know him and that he would have no way of knowing if the person on the other end of the phone was actually Stan. Besides, he wasn't interested in talking to him because it wouldn't prove anything anyway.

Elaine then insisted that Peter call Mary Snodgrass, the therapist who had worked with Stan. As you can imagine, Peter knew something very strange was going on. These people were going to a lot of trouble to convince him that Stan was an unfortunate soul who had been on Prozac and was heavily manipulated at the hands of Preston. The final straw came when Peter pointed out to Mary that Stan could have been brainwashed in prison. Mary said that she was assured by the prison guards that Stan wasn't brainwashed. That was her proof and Peter was very amused. He commented to her that it was good evidence as prison guards have impeccable reputations and are never prone to lie. She agreed and carried on with her conversation, but she missed the sarcasm entirely and lost complete credibility in Peter's eyes.

After getting off the phone with Mary, Peter explained to Elaine that they were digging a deeper hole the more they talked. He even warned them that I might go all out to prove all of this did happen as a result of their trying to convince him. Elaine then blurted out something that was extremely non-sequitur. She said that Stan spoke eight languages and that when his briefcase was confiscated by the CIA en route to Israel that it had been a case of mistaken identity. Peter hadn't heard about the CIA or any trip to Israel and was amazed to hear that Stan spoke so many languages. It occurred to Peter that she might have been programmed or told to deal with some trip Stan took to Israel for the CIA. None of us know what that was about, but it indicates strange business was going on.

Peter returned home and called me that same evening. He insisted on visiting myself and Al Bielek the next day and wanted to get the full scoop on what had happened with Stan. He was now convinced something of a highly irregular nature occurred. He tape recorded the meeting and what you have already read is the edited version of that conversation.

As he was concerned about Stan and his family, he wrote to Stan in prison and asked whether or not he stood by his previous information and wanted his real name in this book. Peter received a strange reply less than a month later. In a carefully worded letter, Stan disavowed any of the information that he had given me. Further, he held me up to ridicule and did not want to be associated with the book in any way. Curiously, he indicated that he had learned the real truth behind the so called Montauk Project and said that he would some day reveal it. If this is so, we would like to know what exactly he learned and who taught it to him!

Stan's letter was read by a few psychics. Although none of them denied that brainwashing did occur, none of them focused on this point. They all focused on the point that Stan was a deeply disturbed individual and had guilt associated with the project.

Peter would speak to Mary Snodgrass once again and would find out that Stan was a model inmate. He was teaching the other prisoners and served in a leadership role. Ironically, it was the same sort of supervisory job that Stan had described for himself at Montauk!

It's now been over a year and Stan was not released from prison as early as normal probation might allow. After all, he was never considered a violent criminal. I believe that he is toeing the line or that he has been worked over heavily. He doesn't want to endanger himself or his family any more than he already has. It will be interesting to see what unfolds when he is finally released from prison. Before he was put away, without any prompting, he swore that he would not recant what he had experienced.

Almost as soon as Stan departed for prison, another oddity began to lurk on the horizon.

14

ALIEN TREATIES

I made a very interesting discovery in 1992 that broke ground for me in understanding how the electronic transistor was developed. This is one other story you won't find in the typical "history of science" textbooks.

First, I will explain the legends of treaties between the Government and different alien groups. These treaties are referred to as legends because there are no copies to show you. I'm not even sure if they exist. I can just tell you what I have heard through the grapevine from countless conversations. The pertinent point, and the only reason I would mention this, is that these legends will serve to help understand the nature of what has occurred with the development of the electronic transistor.

The first treaty between aliens and the U.S. Government was supposedly signed in 1913. I don't have any information on it other than it involved World War I.

The second treaty was signed somewhere around 1945 to 1947. This was supposed to be an alien technology exchange of some kind. Rumor indicated this exchange was with aliens that referred to themselves as the "K Group".

The K Group had been alarmed by the dropping of the atom bomb and wanted the world to disarm from nuclear weapons. They apparently feared what mankind might do. There was an agreement that nuclear devices would be abandoned in return for other technology. Of course, this treaty was not adhered to by the humans and the K Group eventually abandoned us.

The third treaty happened when the Regelian grays came and contacted the Government. These grays said they could help us, but they wanted us to help them as well. They desired certain technology. According to what I'm told, this treaty was agreed upon sometime between 1951 and 1954. We are currently under this treaty although the grays have violated it from time to time.

I believe that alien contact was made in 1946 because of the document which you will see on page 132 entitled "The Surface Barrier Transistor". Notice that it uses the term "crystal valves" in 1946. They were subsequently called the semi-conductor triodes. Finally, in 1948, these devices became known as transistors. This is where my discovery about the transistor begins.

15

THE LEGEND
BEHIND THE TRANSISTOR

The history of the transistor begins with a corporation known as the E.T. Company. It was a fully legal and valid corporation and came into being in the 1950's. You can see their logo on page 131.

There is a gentleman I know who did some lab work at the E.T. Company in about 1960 or '61. I refer to him as Klark, and he is the same Klark that was mentioned in *The Montauk Project: Experiments in Time.* He knows the character Dr. Rinehart who claimed to me that he was John von Neumann, the technical director of the Montauk Project. I also suspect that Klark might keep an eye on Rinehart in a professional intelligence capacity.

I generally believe about 90 percent of what Klark tells me because his stories are sometimes quite fantastic. I'm quite aware that people may say the same thing about myself. This is simply a professional hazard for those who work on or have worked on secret projects.

Klark once told me an interesting story about the E.T. Company. He said that he worked under a gentleman by the name of Herman Anapoly who was also an instructor at RCA Institute (which is now called the Technical

Careers Institute). Anapoly had sworn on a stack of Bibles that in about 1952 or '53, Philco had acquired a government contract from the Navy to set up a special area in the back of the Philco lab. There was extremely high security in this area. Tall thin men dressed in black trench coats were observed to enter the secure area. They also wore odd hats that draped over their faces, leaving holes for two eyes but little else. Anapoly swore to Klark that when they took off their coats and hats, they were actually five foot grays. These aliens taught the personnel to produce a crystal amplifier that became known as the Surface Barrier Transistor.

In an attempt to verify Klark's story, I called the Technical Careers Institute and discovered that there was actually a Herman Anapoly. He taught transistors and at one time was fully employed at the E.T. Company. He eventually retired, started teaching and worked part time at the E.T. Company. So far, Klark's story held together, but it didn't prove alien involvement. It had to be taken with a grain of salt, but I did file it away in my memory. It would prove very significant when a new development took place years later.

16

THE SURFACE
BARRIER TRANSISTOR

In 1984, I made my now famous excursions out to Montauk Point, taking apart various equipment and carting it off piece by piece. As I took things apart, I noticed an oddity. There were about 300 solid state transistors hooked up to the transmitter. This is surprising because solid state technology (which is what transistors are) does not lend itself well to the esoteric technologies with which I was familiar. (For those who are more technically minded, I will say that solid state technology does not lend itself well to the linear amplification of potential etheric technology. Based upon what I knew, I wouldn't have expected any solid state devices to be placed in the analog path of the transmitter). I was familiar with vacuum tubes which are more common when dealing with matters of time and space. To this day, I still do not totally understand the entire setup they had out there.

I yanked out all the little transistor boards and took them home. At the lab, I carefully took the devices off, pulled them out of the mounts and looked at them with a magnifying glass. I recorded the number on the transistor and looked it up in my transistor manual. It said "Type

SB". Referring to the legend in the manual, I discovered that "SB" meant "Surface Barrier". What in the hell was a Surface Barrier? I'd been around electronics a long time and had never heard of it. I was only able to turn up one paper on the Surface Barrier. It turned out to be fifty pages long — a very interesting widget indeed!

My next step was to try and find a Surface Barrier Transistor. I tried to find a Surface Barrier Transistor and called everybody under the sun but was not successful. Finally, I would discover the truth about this device. That occurred in 1992 when I received a call from a Dr. O (fictitious designation). He is a brilliant naturopath and is an expert with cures for AIDS through the use of ozone. He showed up at a Long Island Psychotronics meeting out of the blue and informed us all about the conspiracies concerning AIDS and the medical profession. This is an entire subject all to itself, but it is not the subject of this book. What is significant is that Dr. O invited me to meet a friend of his by the name of Joe Pitone (fictitious name). Joe is a senior executive at Orion Diversified Technologies and was quite friendly. Dr. O thought it would be good for Joe and I to meet each other as we could possibly help each other out.

I was subsequently escorted around the plant and saw a mountain of transistors, diodes and other electronic instruments. Lo and behold - I saw literally millions of Surface Barrier Transistors! I told Joe that I was interested in them as they involved esoteric technology and they would prove useful in my research. He said that we could possibly make some arrangement. I took home a sampling and put them on my tester. These were indeed Surface Barrier Transistors as per the manual.

As I was testing, Duncan walked in the lab and looked at the front page of the catalogue that I'd received from

THE SURFACE-BARRIER TRANSISTOR*

A series of five papers
by members of the technical staff
Philco Research Division

Part I — Principles of the Surface-Barrier Transistor**

W. E. BRADLEY†, FELLOW, IRE

Summary—This paper, consisting of five parts, describes the principle, fabrication, circuit application, and theoretical bases of a new semiconductor transducer, the surface—barrier transistor. This device, produced by precise electrochemical etching and plating techniques, operates at frequencies in excess of 60 mc while displaying the low-voltage, lower-power-consumption and low-noise properties of transistors hitherto confined to much lower frequencies.

Part I describes the basic discovery which led to the new transistor: a new mode of hole injection produced by a broad-area metal electrode in intimate contact with a single crystal of N-type germanium. The mechanisms of hole-emission, conduction, and collection are discussed, and the effect on performance of precise fabrication of germanium sections a few microns in thickness is explained.

Part II describes typical fabrication methods. A germanium blank is etched by directing in its surfaces two opposed jets of a metal salt solution, through which current passes in such polarity as to remove germanium. In addition to etching away material and disposing of the reaction products, the flowing solution cools the work. The etching is allowed to continue until the thickness of the germanium is reduced to a few microns with a tolerance of ±5 per cent of the remaining thickness. A sudden reversal of polarity then stops the etching action and immediately initiates electroplating of metal electrodes from the salt onto the freshly cleaned germanium surfaces.

Part III describes the circuit parameters of the surface-barrier transistor and the performance of typical amplifiers: a compensated video amplifier having a bandwidth of 9 mc and a gain-band width product of 45 mc per stage and a neutralized bandpass rf amplifier centered at 30 mc having an insertion stage gain of 15 db. Switching times in typical switching circuits are less than 0.1 microsecond.

Part IV describes quantitatively the geometrical concepts on which the extended high-frequency performance of the device is based, namely the effect of a flat, thin section of semiconductor between emitter and collector electrodes. Part V gives the theoretical treatment of the basic internal actions of the surface-barrier transistor, hole injection, and hole-current enhancement. Experimental verification of the quantitative predictions of the theory is reported.

INTRODUCTION

IN THE course of research in the Philco Corporation laboratories a new form of transistor, the surface-barrier transistor, has been discovered. This device differs from previously discovered transistors in that it contains only one form of germanium, whereas earlier devices contained at least two forms. Alloy junction transistors, for example, are described as p-n-p or n-p-n types, while the point-contact transistors has regions of modified germanium produced by the forming process

---

* The research leading to the development of the surface-barrier transistor was supported in part by the Bureau of Ships, Department of the Navy, under Contract NObsr 57322.

** Decimal classification: R282.12. Original manuscript received by the Institute, October 14, 1953.

† Philco Corp., Research Div., Philadelphia, Pa.

near the point contacts. The new surface-barrier transistor is an N-type transistor.

The name "Surface-Barrier Transistor" is derived from the fact that the interfaces of the transistor which perform the functions of emission and collection of the useful current are located at *the surface* of a uniform crystal-base electrode. The development of an active interface located at the crystal surface results in a new mode of operation upon the charge carriers of the crystal permitting the use of metal electrodes of relatively large area.

The fact that the electrodes are applied to the surface of the crystal after the crystal has been shaped permits accurate control of the geometry of the transistor to a degree unheard of in prior art. Accurately controlled fabrication of N-type germanium in sections of a few microns in thickness is readily achieved, for example, by the electrochemical techniques described by Tiley and Williams.[1]

The practical result of this new principle and the associated techniques is a transistor of unprecedented performance characteristics. Efficient operation on a power supply of three volts of less at frequencies above 60 nmegacycles has been achieved and substantially higher frequency operation is anticipated with further refinement of the fabrication method. Band-pass amplification centered at a frequency of 30 megacycles has been demonstrated and low-pass amplification from zero to 9 megacycles has been achieved. In brief, the surface barrier transistor combines low-voltage, low-power-consumption, low-noise-figure operation at frequencies higher by more than an order of magnitude than can be attained with available alloy-junction transistors.

The principles and techniques embodied in the surface-barrier stransistor are applicable not only to the particular type described herein but also to other forms as those familiar with the art will readily appreciate from the detailed description of the electrochemical technique in the associated paper[1]

THE SURFACE BARRIER OF N-TYPE GERMANIUM

The useful current of the surface-barrier transistor is a current of holes moving from the emitter to the collector. The free electrons which are normally present in

---

[1] PROC. I.R.E., pp. 1706-1708; this issue.

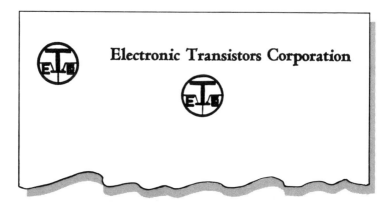

Electronic Transistors Corporation

Orion Diversified Technologies Inc.
6 Cherry Street • ▆▆▆▆▆, L.I., N.Y. 117▆▆
Telephone (516)▆▆▆▆▆▆ • Fax (516)▆▆▆▆▆

LETTERHEADS

At the top of the page is the letterhead for the E.T. Company.
They produced virtually all the transistors in the U.S. during the 1950's
which were resold by many different distributors.
The company eventually had financial difficulty and adopted
the name Orion Diversified Technologies.
Their letterhead is also shown above.
Orion moved from the Cherry Street
address many years ago.

Joe. It said "E.T. Co." He thought that I'd concocted some sort of joke and that "E.T." was meant to stand for "Extra-terrestrial". I told him no, that is the name of a real company. Suddenly, I remembered what my friend Klark had told me about working for the E.T. Company. I called him immediately.

"Yes, that's the name of the company I worked for." Klark said.

All along, Klark had been giving me more information than the papers on the Surface Barrier Transistor revealed. He obviously knew more. This also validated his story that he had actually worked on them in the 1960's. He basically analyzed them and tested them in the lab.

Klark also related stories from that era. He said that the company joke of the day was that "E.T." stood for "Extra-Terrestrial". I reminded him about the story of Herman Anapoly saying that aliens had worked on the transistors. Klark swore that Anapoly had indeed said this was true.

I asked Duncan to do a reading on the transistors and he said that they were the key to opening the time barrier. There was also free energy, sometimes referred to as Tachyon energy, in the transistors.

In addition to Duncan, I called Al Bielek in Phoenix and asked him to do a reading on the transistors. He hadn't been told any information from the earlier reading. I was keeping things very quiet because I didn't want to say anything until I could have the devices under my control. I was afraid some competitor might try to buy them all up.

Al indicated that the transistors went right back to the alien technology exchange. He said the original alien device was in a plastic package about a half an inch in diameter and had eight leads coming out of it. It consisted of six of these SBTs ganged together in one packet. His

133

read said literally that the aliens had come to us because they were having reliability troubles with these things in their craft. The SBTs drove the levitation of the power crystal. Now, it all began to make sense. A spacecraft requires free energy and control of gravitational waves. If you're dealing with these factors, you've literally got to have an opening into space and time. This is exactly where the SBT fit in.

It is also interesting to note that I was pronouncing Joe Pitone's name incorrectly. When I had spoken to Klark, he corrected me on the pronunciation. This convinced me completely that Klark had worked at the E.T. Company and that he in fact knew Joe Pitone. Klark asked that I not mention him to Joe.

I went back to see Joe Pitone and said that I had a friend who worked for the E.T. Company quite some time ago. I told him the story about the initials of "E.T." standing for "Extra-Terrestrial". I asked if it were true and he got almost bug-eyed. He was silent and bug-eyed for about a minute. I knew then that I'd struck a nerve. He finally admitted that it had been a major rumor. He said that he didn't know if it was true.

About two hours later I went to him again and said, "Come on, Joe, tell me. Is the alien involvement in E.T. Company true?"

He said, "Yes, it is, Preston".

17

HISTORY OF THE ELECTRONIC TRANSISTOR

After Joe admitted ET involvement with the company, I proceeded to do some corporate research. I looked at the corporate structure of the E.T. Company and found out that they started as a bunch of rebels. They flourished and built up quite a business. Eventually they acquired too many bean counters and went into Chapter 11 bankruptcy. Joe, being the major stockholder, ended up with the company in his hands. He reorganized it and renamed the company Orion Diversified Technologies.

The next thing I sought to find out was where did the name "Orion Diversified" come from. This was very suspicious as legends had persisted that the alien group from Montauk was from Orion. The reptilian race from Orion is also popular in much New Age literature. Whatever the case, there is no denying that there is a real company that is actually named "Orion Diversified" which grew out of the original E.T. Company. It is all a matter of legal record. Joe claimed that his daughter actually made up the name "Orion" for the company. To me, all of this is too much to be a coincidence. Although the name is very tongue in cheek, it is a further indication of alien involvement.

Now, if we look at the bottom of the first page in the first column of "Surface Barrier Transistors", we see at the top of the footnotes: "The research leading to the development of the Surface Barrier Transistor was supported in part by the Bureau of Ships, Dept. of Navy under contract number, etc." For those who don't know, common legend has it that the alien technology exchange is supposed to filter through the Navy. The Navy applies the technology exchange through the Naval Research Laboratory. This fits in as one more piece of the puzzle.

If we look at the original manuscript on the SBT, we find that it was received on October 14, 1953. I consulted several UFO experts that I know and asked what happened about this time period. They uniformly said that a year earlier, in the summer of 1952, the White House was buzzed by a massive fleet of UFOs. This is documentable history and is even reported in the newspapers of the period although they have a tendency to water down the sightings considerably. There are pictures though and a serious researcher will find convincing evidence. The buzzing happened for a while and then ceased. The Earth was then contacted once again by the aliens. It is at this point that they gave us the Surface Barrier Transistor.

Now, let's go back to the genesis of the transistor. Crystal valves (or amplifiers) came out in 1946 from Great Britain. The transistor as we know it today came out in 1947. This was occasioned by a discovery at Bell Labs. The key scientists who claimed the discovery were named Shockley, Pearson and Hayes. A man named Osborne headed a group of people who were invaluable in marketing the transistor.

If we go to the last page of the Surface Barrier information, we see the transistor semi-conductor triode came out in 1948. There is an interesting time sequence here.

Next, let's assume that we did pop off the first atomic bombs and the K Group aliens got very upset about it. What would they do about it? Threaten Truman? More likely, they would have told the President that they didn't want him to make any more bombs and to abandon the project entirely. The K Group would have offered a new technology to replace the atomic efforts but still place the U.S. as the world leader. A treaty was then signed for an alien technology exchange.

The first order of business was to get away from the cumbersome vacuum tube. The Government took the project up to ATT Bell Labs so that their think tank could have a look and do some research. The aliens showed Shockley and company how to take a compact diode, use it as a detector and eventually make it into a crystal amplifier. Keep in mind that the early name for the transistor was a crystal valve.

I have some very early transistors in my collection which are designated as "221's". These are one of the very first transistors. They come packed in a little cardboard case. On it, it says "military part #221, crystal amplifier". It does not say transistor. This was made in 1946.

How did the name "transistor" come about?

Shockley and his crowd developed the crystal valve (the basics being supplied by aliens) so that it was easily reproducible and fully marketable. This seemed to be their main contribution. Osborne handled the business end and spun off the first company that would market transistors. These partners chose the name "E.T. Company" believing that the alien contact was going to be common news after a few years. When that happened, the name of the company would be changed to the "Extra-Terrestrial Company" and they would have a monopoly on that name. Osborne wanted to play on that, but they weren't going to call it "Extra-Terrestrial" to start off with. They couldn't yet claim they were E.T. based so they brainstormed for names that used the initials "E.T." The "E" was easy. That could stand for "electronic". "T" required a little more imagination. A crystal valve is sort of like a translator and sort of a like a resistor. The word "translator" doesn't quite fit. Instead, they came up with the word "transistor" (translator + resistor) because it starts with a "t" and also describes the object.

In researching this, I found out that no one had the facilities to manufacture transistors. There was only one exception and this was a group in Orange, New Jersey. I found out the original plant the E.T. Company used was the Western Electric plant that was used for making semiconductors. This is all very interesting because Western Electric was a major contractor to the Navy for the Philadelphia Experiment. Osborne had actually helped to start up and then spin off a manufacturing division of Western Electric. The name "Electronic Transistor Company" was incorporated at the outset because they didn't want to be accused of having a monopoly as Western Electric.

By the early 1950's, the E.T. Company had come alive and was making transistors for everybody. Bell Labs introduced the transistor through their channels. The Institute of Radio Engineers which today is the Institute of Electric and Electronic Engineers, did the same. This list goes on and on. The E.T. Company made the transistors and the others sold them.

Subsequent to this, the E.T. Company was given information on how to make point contact transistors and what are known as alloy transistors. This bolstered their business for a while but the company would eventually run into trouble of a most unusual nature.

18

ALIEN TECHNOLOGY EXCHANGE AND THE ORION CONNECTION

As the transistor industry developed, the Government continued to make atomic bombs and build up the nuclear arsenal. Eventually, the K Group showed up and they were understandably very upset. They wanted to know what was going on. The K Group was told by the Government that nuclear weapons were needed to keep the upper hand in the world situation. They wanted to have their cake and eat it, too. Atomic power and the alien technology exchange meant not only military domination of the world but superior electronic technology. The K Group was not pleased and left. Fortunately for us, they weren't hostile.

The Government's decisions in these matters is certainly open to criticism, however their choices had been complicated by the Roswell crash of 1947. There, the military had discovered human body parts in an alien craft. This was not the K Group, but Truman was reported to be very upset. What were these "advanced beings" doing with human body parts?

The Roswell craft was studied, at least what was left

of it. There were actually two crafts and one was somewhat intact. They learned what frequencies the aliens communicated at and also some of the alien language. Big radio transmitters were turned on and the military kept sending out the communication, "We want to talk to you."

The next thing that happened was that the sightings became more numerous and crafts were seen flying about Washington. The aliens indicated a willingness to talk and there was a meeting. Truman wanted to know why they were picking up body parts. I believe the aliens gave an excuse. They might have said something to the effect that they were trying to clone a human.

An agreement was reached that included the technology exchange. The aliens had trouble with some of the equipment on their ships and they wanted to find someone in the galaxy who could produce equipment for them. This equipment primarily consisted of the Surface Barrier Transistor. The aliens would receive a cheap and effective labor source and the humans would get alien technology. That is the point in the story when the Regelian Greys appear in the plant.

The story I got from Joe Pitone was that the production of the SBTs would stop, start up again, stop and follow this sort of pattern.

Al Bielek worked at Singer HRV. He remembers them making some kind of weird electronic counter measure receiver that used the Surface Barrier Transistor. While he was there, Singer called up their supplier, the Sprage Company, to order some more SBTs. Suddenly, they were not available. What had happened?

Investigation showed that it was Sprage that actually had a major contract with the Government to sell the SBTs. This contract had been subcontracted out to the E.T. Company. Sprage had been ordered to shut down the entire line. Not only could Singer not get their SBTs, the E.T. Company was now stuck with a half billion transistors that they had already produced for the purpose of Sprage's government contract. They had unsalable merchandise on their hands and were told to scrap it. The E.T. Company wanted to be compensated for what they had produced and decided they could change the number on the SBTs and sell them under their own name. They were told by the Government that they couldn't do that, and if they did, they would be held in treason.

The E.T. Company was understandably upset and negotiations continued. It was finally decided that Sprage would pay the E.T. Company for all costs to produce the transistors. They would then be destroyed or scrapped as per the Government's direction. In a cabalistic turnaround, meetings were held at the E.T. Company. They surprisingly decided that the transistors would be shelved and put away for a rainy day. The Government would assume they had been destroyed.

The company eventually ended up in Chapter 11 bankruptcy. That means the company is protected from its creditors so that it can reorganize its management and become viable. The company was renamed Orion Diversified and Joe remained as a key executive. The company has since emerged out of bankruptcy and is functioning as a government contractor once again.

I was introduced to Joe as the company was getting its act together. The SBTs were still in storage and Joe asked me to have a look at them. I took some home and asked Duncan to do a reading on them. He said that these transistors were key to bending time because of their esoteric properties. We would need about 150,000 of them. According to Duncan's reading, these were part and parcel of a time machine. I also discovered that the SBTs

141

had healing properties that were even stronger than the Tachyon energy beads that are popular in Japan. These properties were demonstrated with kinesiological testing by Bernice Louie at a Long Island Psychotronics meeting.

I went back to Joe and told him I would like to have as many transistors as possible. These were still a hot item as far as the Government was concerned and he seemed anxious for me to have them. I worked for him in an engineering capacity for several weeks and we had agreed to work out some sort of barter arrangement. My time would compensate for the transistors.

Within a short time, a bushel of transistors were missing from his warehouse. What happened next continues an even stranger mystery. It is best not told by myself.

PART
III

BY PETER MOON

III

INTRODUCTION
TO PART III

The fact that Preston even met Joe Pitone was highly ironic. The working relationship eventually abated but the time period was highly dramatic and was not easy for Preston to deal with. In hindsight, it appears someone was setting a trap for Preston in an effort to bring him back into the Montauk fold.

I will relay what happened with Orion Diversified as I found myself in the middle of the fireworks for a short period of time. This will be followed by corroborations of the Montauk Project and further experiences that have occurred from that time until the completion of this book (Summer, 1993).

19

ORION COMES ALIVE

I first heard about Joe Pitone shortly after *The Montauk Project* was first published. Preston had given a lecture at the Long Island Psychotronics chapter on the subject of the Surface Barrier Transistor. He also talked about Joe and the E.T. Company.

Shortly after the lecture, Preston called and informed me that someone was interested in doing a movie. My first reaction was that this was all extremely premature. I definitely expected to see this story taken to the screen but this was too quick. The book was hardly in the book stores at that point. I asked him who the interest was coming from, and he told me that it was from Joe Pitone and a certain Dr. O. This sounded almost comical to me as they are far from being professional movie makers. Preston also told me that a major director had read the book and the projected cost to make the movie right might be $50,000,000. Preston also explained that Joe is worth about $50,000,000 on paper. He owns many different companies and is juggling things all the time. This was paper worth though and certain deals would have to come through before he could cash out. This also seemed very odd. If someone had fifty million, why would they want to

147

invest it all in a risky adventure like a motion picture?

I was already suspicious of Joe because of Preston's story about the transistor. My main concern was that someone might try to buy the rights to the picture and never release it. This is a common axiom in Hollywood: buy up and suppress movies that express the truth or expand the consciousness and put out schlock.

By this time, I had also become friends with Dr. O. He showed up at a Psychotronics meeting one night but wouldn't give me his name or tell me where he lived, only that he came from Florida. I would later find out that he was security conscious about the ozone machines he sells. As mentioned earlier, ozone is purported to be extremely effective in the treatment of AIDS and Dr. O is always looking over his shoulder for the FDA or AMA. The machines are sold only as water or air purifiers and they are expressly forbidden to be used for the treatment of any disease. For some strange reason (probably because it works!), people use them to treat diseases. Dr. O doesn't do anything illegal by selling the ozone machines as purifiers, but he is ever cautious. His friend, a valid medical doctor, has a clinic in a foreign country that administers ozone treatments. This friend was shot at and his house was burned to the ground. Consequently, you can understand Dr. O's hestitancy to reveal personal information about himself.

I got to know Dr. O by advising him on how to publish a manuscript he had written. I also found him to be the most knowledgeable person I'd ever met as far as knowing effective treatments against bodily afflictions. His information resulted in medical miracles for me and my family which I will not elaborate on. Consequently, he became a good friend.

It seemed very odd to me that Dr. O suddenly showed

up at Psychotronics and introduced Preston to Joe Pitone, the man who just happens to have all these surface barrier transistors. I told Dr. O that this was too much of a coincidence when you put all of the other circumstances together. Dr. O just laughed and said that Joe is just a regular guy and doesn't have any "strange" connections. He said that Joe was a boarder in his mother's house when they were much younger.

Preston set up an appointment for me to meet with him and Joe in order to discuss the movie rights for *The Montauk Project*. Upon meeting Joe, the first spontaneous thought that ran through my head was that this man was an alien. That was a totally subjective thought — it just came out in my mind. I didn't vocalize it to him.

Joe is in his 70's and looks very good for his age. He can be quite a gentleman and is also an excellent story teller. As he spoke about his interest in the movie, it came across totally differently than what had been told to me previously. He was interested in acquiring the rights to the movie and showing it on his balance sheet as an asset for reasons that are too complex to go into. A quick payout could probably have been arranged, but neither Preston nor myself were eager to make a deal. Joe made it clear that he is not a movie maker, but that he has connections to Orion Pictures. I pointed out that Orion Pictures was under Chapter 11 bankruptcy proceedings. He acknowledged this was true and told an interesting story. Joe said that Orion Diversified emerged out of Chapter 11 bankruptcy after court proceedings on April 29, 1992. The next court docket that day was Orion Pictures entering into Chapter 11 bankruptcy. He claimed there was no connection between the two companies. The synchronicity in these matters is certainly odd. He just happens to know executives at Orion Pictures!

Joe went into the possibilities and options in detail and he definitely seemed knowledgeable about such matters. He said that if he couldn't get involved in it directly, he would at least help us make the best possible deal. Supposedly, Orion's bankruptcy (which they have since emerged from) wouldn't hurt the deal. Things could be structured so that there would be no liability of the movie not being made. We all agreed to keep talking and while interest in a movie has been generated from Japan and in other quarters, nothing has happened with Orion or Joe Pitone. But something of a far more intriguing nature was beginning to develop.

20

MONTAUK COMES ALIVE

Earlier, it was mentioned that a bushel full of surface barrier transistors was found missing from Orion Diversified. This had happened just before I had visited the plant. While, I was there, Preston gave me a tour and took me to a work bench in the corner. There was a piece of paper which had written on it, "We can get in any time we want".

This indicated that someone was playing games. Presumably, some faction of the secret government knew Orion had these contraband transistors and were flexing their muscle. There was no evidence of break in so this was either a high security job or a teleportation.

In the meantime, Joe had given Preston a tremendous amount of SBTs. He wanted Preston to test them and tell him which ones were good and exactly what sense he could make out of them. According to Preston's story, a barter arrangement was to be worked out whereby Preston's time would be paid for by giving him SBTs, at a price to be determined later. At this point, Preston discovered that these transistors possessed Tachyon energy. This means that they had healing powers. Anyone who is at all sensitive can notice a definite vibration that these transistors give off when they are held. They have been tested on many different people. Preston actually analyzed them and determined how they were made. (He considers this proprietary information so please don't ask for the formula).

After Preston's discovery, all hell seemed to break loose. Suddenly a huge misunderstanding arose. Orion suspected Preston of having taken transistors that Preston understood he was supposed to keep in lieu of payment.

Preston was mystified as to what was going on. He knew I was friendly with Dr. O and asked me to talk to him and get a feel for Joe's position. I subsequently invited Dr. O to my house and we had the first of what were to be many bizarre conversations.

As he sat in a lawn chair, he mentioned that he had been reading the *Montauk Pioneer* and noticed a review of *The Montauk Project* in it. The *Montauk Pioneer* is a small weekly that has extremely limited circulation.

"How did you get a copy of that paper?" I asked.

He told me that he got it out at Montauk. I asked him what in the hell he was doing out there, and he explained that he goes out there all the time. This is about a two and a half hour ride so I wanted to know why he went out there. He said he liked to pick the grapes out there because they are excellent. This was almost as funny as it was weird. I pointed to an abundance of grapes in my own yard and told him he wouldn't have to go out there anymore. He could pick all he wanted.

Dr. O then surprised me again by telling me that he also goes out there to visit his wife. This was odd because his wife lived with him and her job was nearby. Why would she go out to Montauk? He said she liked to go out there, rent a motel and just visit because it was so nice. I would later find out there was a woman who fit Dr. O's wife's description that worked as a bartender on the base when it was functioning. She had the same first name and was the same age, but I have not been able to establish whether they are one and the same person.

I presented the whole scenario to Dr. O and said I thought it was extremely odd that he showed up out of nowhere and just happened to connect up Preston with Orion Diversified and all these top secret transistors. He emphatically denied that there was anything unusual or secretive about Joe Pitone. I pointed out that Joe had connections to the carting industry (garbage) on Long Island. And for those who do not know, anyone in the New York area who deals in the carting industry had better be approved or sanctioned by the mob. If you don't believe me, trying opening up a competitive business and see what happens.

Dr. O acknowledged that Joe had connections in this regard but that he clearly stayed away from any illegal activities. He also said that Joe was a heavy mover and shaker as far as politics were concerned and could get things done. Still, Dr. O wouldn't bite at my suggestion that all of this indicated an even stranger involvement.

I continued to be quite frank with Dr. O. I told him that I'd even asked a psychic (that I know to be accurate although not foolproof) to read on his own involvement. This psychic indicated that Dr. O was a dupe and was being used on some level. He thought that was amusing and said that maybe he was a dupe and maybe it was all being done in an alternate reality. We have joked about this ever since, but he has yet to explain the oddities mentioned.

Dr. O was of the opinion that Preston had stolen the transistors. Although it was not their intention to do so, he said that Preston could be put in jail. I thought this was hilarious because if the transistors were contraband, a court case could get very messy indeed.

This whole situation between Preston and Orion Diversified was much more weird and emotional than I will relay here. I found myself hearing stories from both sides which contrasted considerably. The most notable difference between the two parties was that Preston was willing to consider all possibilities. He was distraught by it all and wanted some answers. Orion, on the other hand, through the mouthpiece of Dr. O, was very coy. Their position was that Preston was just making things up. It is too easy to accuse him of that. All of this points to strange and concealed information from Orion.

At one point in the conversation with Dr. O, I told him of an encounter Preston had during this time period. One night, Preston returned to his house to find a man waiting in a car. This man claimed to be from the Government. He told Preston that they wanted him back. They had lost most of their time capability and while they could view different times on monitors, they could not keep things stable enough for travelling purposes. Preston told him that he had been screwed over once before and didn't want to have anything to do with it. The man was not forceful but left an open invitation.

I then told Dr. O that Preston had received an offer from the Government to purchase the SBTs at a price of $25 per transistor. I did not think that Dr. O would believe me, but he fired back that Orion had been offered about $13 per transistor. Here again is another oddity: the Government buying back material that they could supposedly confiscate! Preston does not remember the offer from the Government although I have it in my notes and remember him telling me.

I didn't quite know what to make of all this. I did some serious thinking about Dr. O and marvelled at his unique medical knowledge. He is truly incredible and is literally light years ahead of the medical world. It occurred to me that if one had the reins of the Montauk Project and could command tremendous resources, they would likely have the best medical care available and that it would far surpass medical technology of today. Now, Dr. O began to make a little more sense.

After telling him my thesis, Dr. O sort of smiled but took no credit. He obviously liked the compliment, but he was more interested to find out whether or not Preston took the job at Montauk. I told him no and that there was no way he should. We debated the issue. Dr. O seemed to think that if the technology of time could be properly harnessed, there could be great gifts for man. This might be true, but you'd first have to trust the powers that be. We do not.

The final chapter on this whole episode is not ready to be written yet and it leaves more questions than answers. The misunderstandings between Preston and Orion Diversified that were referred to previously have since been ironed out and there is no animosity between any of the players here.

Dr. O continues to play cat and mouse, yet he is always there when I need him for something. His latest claim is interesting. He said he met a gentleman who just happened to be flying an airplane on August 12, 1943 and remembers seeing the *U.S.S. Eldridge* disappear as a blip on the radar screen. According to Dr. O, this man also invented the beefalo, which is an interesting genetic development from decades ago. This is a laboratory cross breeding of buffalo and cattle. What is even more interesting is that Dr. O says he will be meeting the man who was in charge of the genetic experiments at Montauk.

And what is last, but not least, Dr. O has given me

scientific descriptions of how to reverse the aging process and keep the body from dying. This is a whole other story in itself and would require considerable time and study on my part. Immortality and time travel might be fun, but they also require a lot of hard work.

21

A VISIT TO VON NEUMANN

There is never a dull moment around Space Time Labs. As soon as the scenario surrounding the Surface Barrier Transistors was cooling down, Preston asked me if I'd like to go up and meet his friend Klark and Dr. Rinehart, the man who had once claimed to Preston that he was John von Neumann. He was concerned that Rinehart might die and thought it would be important for me to chronicle that the guy actually existed. If I was lucky, he might even reveal himself to me as von Neumann.

After a very long drive, we arrived at a country lot surrounded by woods. There was a good size trailer with garbage strewn about the yard. It looked more like a junk yard than a dwelling. Dr. Rinehart was outside and recognized Preston, although he knows him by a different name. He came over and was quite friendly but was very odd. He does resemble von Neumann's pictures to some degree, but due to his advanced age, it's hard to say whether he is or not. Besides, it's possible that von Neumann's spirit was placed in the body so that genetics are not the ultimate test.

Preston had warned me not to mention anything of a metaphysical nature to this man because he would react poorly to it. I was introduced as a World War II researcher who was particularly interested in Navy ships. Preston then talked about mundane matters and tried to help him with some of his personal and financial problems.

Rinehart appears to be more like a homeless sorry soul than a doctor of anything. He has no heat for his trailer and seems to live off the largesse of General Electric who mysteriously show up whenever he has a piece of electronic equipment to sell. Rinehart has no phone, so he writes a letter to G.E. Someone then comes out, treats him very nicely and buys the equipment. It is possible they do this in lieu of a formal pension but no one is quite sure. And although he could easily pass for a derelict, Rinehart is as sharp as a tack when it comes to the subjects of electronics and radio. You wouldn't believe that someone who seems so despondent in general could be so responsive on a subject that is so complex and exact.

We tried to steer the conversation toward 1943 and the Rainbow Project. I asked him directly if he remembered it. He said that he'd heard about it back then but didn't know much about it. Preston asked him about the contractors from the time period such as Western Electric and he seemed to recall a great deal about all of them. In fact, Rinehart's memories of people and events were astounding and it even went back years. I told him he had a photographic memory, and he said that people often tell him that.

When Rinehart went off to talk to some people who were interested in his property, Preston indicated that his memories were too good. In fact, he sounded like someone who had been programmed to remember things. I specifically asked him about Tesla, and he fondly recounted the Father of Radio. But what he said sounded like he'd memorized a page blurb from Tesla's biography. It really sounded suspicious. Then, he surprised us both by saying that he remembered seeing

Tesla's free energy tower (which was never completed) at what is now Shoreham, Long Island. This was odd, as he would have been about 13 at the time it was torn down. I pointed out that he would have had to have seen it as a youngster, but he couldn't remember when he'd seen it, only that he had seen it.

Probably the only other significant thing Rinehart talked about was his family. He said that his brother had worked on the Joint Chiefs of Staff and was somewhat adversarial with him. From what he said, it was clear that his personal family was neck deep in the military and defense industry.

The conversation rambled around for hours, and I grew impatient to leave. He'd only appeared as von Neumann to Preston. No one else had reported seeing this side of the man, and there was no great anticipation that he would come out for me. Then, as we said good-bye, he looked at me and winked.

He said, "Next time you come up here, I'll tell you about some secret radio projects!"

Overall, the trip to Dr. Rinehart was inconclusive. It didn't prove Preston's contention that he is von Neumann, but there is definitely something very weird and unexplained about this character. He did act like he was programmed, and his family background fit the bill for an identity relocation program. Hopefully, I will meet him again soon and he will tell me some real secrets.

22

A VISIT TO KLARK

After our visit with Dr. Rinehart, we drove for several miles and met up with Klark. He was mentioned in *The Montauk Project* as the man who introduced Preston to Rinehart.

Klark lives in a well shaded and beautiful area that is very peaceful and far away from the city. Upon our arrival, we sat down at a picnic table and began to discuss whether it would be too chilly to stay outside. I then made a comment that it was too bad we didn't have some radiosondes so that we could change the weather. Klark looked me right in the eye and said that the weather can definitely be changed. He said it with an absolute certainty. I now got a much different impression of him than when I'd been introduced. He acted like brass. By that, I mean brass in the armed forces. My guess was that he had served at Montauk on the highest level.

I got to know him generally and found out he has all sorts of interesting contraptions, some of which he stores for Preston. He literally believes that Preston will build a time machine because he remembers being visited by him (Preston from the future) in the past. Consequently, Klark finds pieces of the time machine now and then and either gives them to Preston or holds on to them until the time is right to pass them on.

Klark could be considered unusual because of the above but he is not a fool. He's an extremely serious person and holds down an important job in the field of medical technology, in addition to having more than a layman's knowledge of electronics. If this doesn't make him a candidate for Montauk involvement, his family is loaded with Defense Department connections as well. Upon meeting Klark, it occurred to me that Montauk is not only a real scenario but that it is filled with real life players.

Preston informed me that Klark does not open up often to others, but he surprised us both by telling me that he had seen himself as an older man when he was a youngster. It was a paradox, and he wasn't in denial about it.

Now, I'd met another time traveller besides Duncan and Al Bielek. I sensed however that Klark might have used Duncan in the processes of Montauk. In other words, Duncan was the guinea pig who was utilized to open the portals and was also stripped psychicly. Klark was one who received the "benefit" of travelling in time but at a cost to Duncan. None of this is meant to put Klark down. It's not even foolproof true as it's only my perception of the role he probably played. But it is interesting to note that Duncan can't stand to be around either Klark or Dr. Rinehart. It apparently brings up too many bad memories. It's nothing personal on Duncan's part. It should also be pointed out that Klark has his problems with the Government. They've not made his life easy, and he believes they have caused or contributed to a terminal cancer condition with his wife.

Klark was happy with *The Montauk Project* and mentioned that he'd like to help with some further books. He definitely had a specific agenda in mind for all this and exactly how the movie should be done. He wanted to use the profits to help assemble a time machine. At one point, it sounded like he was giving me orders but this did not become an issue. He continues to speak with Preston on a routine basis, but so far he hasn't offered any further information.

In an interesting development that took place after my meeting with Klark, Preston was paid a visit by Brian's mother. Brian, to refresh your memory, was Preston's psychic assistant in the first book when he made the initial trip out to Montauk. She had visited Preston's place while Klark just happened to be there and was in for the shock of her life. Klark looked just like Brian! Apparently, Brian was Klark and there was time travelling going on. It was more confusing than logical to all parties concerned, including Preston. I, of course, wanted to meet Brian and his mother. Preston is open to it, but we have not yet been able to reach them at this writing.

23

A VISIT WITH HELGA MORROW

About a month after I visited Dr. Rinehart and Klark, I received a call from Helga Morrow. She remembered the Philadelphia Experiment and the Montauk Project because her father, Dr. Frederich A. Kueppers, had worked on both of them. Helga's story is very interesting and serves as one more corroboration that there was a Montauk Project.

In 1981, she attended a dinner party and was introduced to a Dr. so-and-so. Helga asked if he was a Ph.D. or an M.D. and was told that he had a Ph.D. in engineering. She mentioned that her father also had a similar degree and that he'd worked for the Glenn L. Martin Company (now Martin-Marietta). When this man heard that she was talking about Dr. Kueppers, he was astonished. He confided to her that her father had been one of the scientists who had worked on the Philadelphia Experiment. He had also invented the timing device for the A-bomb (and represented the scientists to President Truman, asking him not to drop it), invented the mathematical formula that brought the astronauts back, and designed the miniaturized electrical system of the Sputnik. In addition to those accomplishments, he worked on Project Blue Book/Black Book (UFOs), initiated the use of aluminum wiring to replace heavier wiring in WW II planes, and worked with mind warfare, including the use of psychics to communicate with astronauts in case of communications systems failure. He even trained extraterrestrials to fit into human society.

Suddenly, everything began to make sense for Helga. She was born in 1935 in Baltimore. During the gestation process, her mother's gynecologist, a noted spiritualist by the name of Dr. Haase, inserted a mysterious metallic rod into the womb in order to enhance the I.Q. and psychic ability of Helga. She was a government experiment! To this day, you can see what appears to be an antenna structure in X-ray pictures of her head. This is part of what makes her an acute sensitive and psychic.

Helga recalled early experiences with her father. He even showed her how two objects could transpose in time and return the same way. Taking her to the cellar, he put steel shavings in a cigar box with a large U-shaped magnet taped underneath. Gently tapping the shavings, two concentric circles gradually appeared. He said that if one could transpose the circles, one could actually change time. According to Dr. Kueppers, alien spacecraft were partly moved by reverse magnetism and he showed her how to create this effect by holding two opposite magnets.

His interest in time fits into perspective through an interesting story. When August 12th arrived one year, Dr. Kueppers took Helga aside and told her it was a very special day. This did not surprise her as it was her mother's birthday. Dr. Kueppers indicated that was very important but that he was referring to something of much greater magnitude for mankind. He said it was the anniversary of a very great experiment that he had been a part of.

Helga also remembers being taken as a child into an underground facility in Colorado with her father. She went down several floors in an elevator, entered into a high security area and saw photos of men on the moon and what appeared to be shuttle craft similar to today's. That was in the 1950's

Dr. Kueppers believed that the Russian and American scientists had worked in collaboration for years and that the cold war was a sham. In fact, he became such a rebel that he was finally put away and electrically shocked into submission. His death certificate was issued in 1962, but Helga noticed that the man in the coffin was not her father. It was a scam. All of this was a puzzle to Helga and she didn't know what to make of it until she one day saw a paper by her father that was written in the 1970's. The language was German and the leak was unanticipated.

Helga was seeking her father or any information about him and that brought her to Long Island in January of 1993. I introduced her to Preston and Duncan and we all went to dinner. We were also accompanied by Al Bielek who has known Helga for some time. The dinner was interesting and Preston said he'd met her father at Brookhaven. He didn't remember too much about him and this seemed unfortunate. We then returned to Space-Time Labs and she became very emotional about her father. Duncan and Helga then proceeded to do some trance readings. Preston went out the door for about five minutes and suddenly returned. He announced that he had just had a download from a Pleidian data base and rattled off all sorts of information about Dr. Kueppers. We were all astonished that Helga said much of the information was accurate. The rest of it was unfamiliar to her so she couldn't confirm or deny it. As Preston channeled the information, he also had a memory breakthrough from Montauk. Dr. Kueppers had indeed worked at Montauk and Preston even remembered the exact door with the initials "F.A.K." on them. Sadly, Preston indicated that Dr. Kueppers was no longer with us. He was a passionate scientist and although he despised the politics, he was thrilled to exercise his knowledge on secret projects. Unfortunately, his love for science cost him his freedom and eventually his life.

Helga went out to Montauk the next day and went to the office that had been her father's. Although the door had been blown off or otherwise removed, she was sure it was his office. The rest of the day was also interesting. Video shots were taken of the area and an underground bunker was also visited. A cage was found that allegedly housed the Montauk boys prior to their programming. It was a very gruesome sight and so horrified Duncan that he broke down and cried over his involvement in the project, apologizing profusely.

After her visit to Long Island, Helga travelled to Maryland to visit a family associate who decades earlier had been instrumental in getting their father committed. From conversations she'd had with him, Helga knew the basement of his house contained papers that might reveal proof of some of the projects Dr. Kueppers was involved in. Unfortunately, he wouldn't let her in the house.

Perhaps the most amusing and ironic story Helga relayed was that of Dr. John von Neumann. He used to be a frequent dinner guest to the Kueppers' home in the 1940's. She said that he had a real sweet tooth and one of his favorite desserts was strawberry ice cream. Ironically, this just happens to be the favorite of Dr. Rinehart!

Helga is currently working on a book. Hopefully, she will discover more answers to the mystery of her father.

24

THE NORFOLK TRIPLETS

About the same time I met Helga, we received a letter from another lady who claimed her father had been involved in the Philadelphia Experiment. She sent along a newspaper clipping from the *Norfolk Virginian-Pilot* that included a short article and a photo of a set of triplets that were born in February of 1945. This lady was one of the triplets and referred to herself as "Baby A", her sisters being "Baby B" and "Baby C". While she told me her real name, she asked that it be kept confidential for the book.

The newspaper article indicated their father was a radio mechanic at the Norfolk Naval Operating Base. This is noteworthy because according to the literature on the Philadelphia Experiment, the *U.S.S. Eldridge* had teleported to waters off the coast of Norfolk, Virginia. Baby A thought it was odd that her father was listed as a mere radio mechanic because he travelled by jet and was saluted by military personnel even though he wore blue collar garb.

According to family information, the father had been expecting the *U.S.S. Eldridge* during the Philadelphia Experiment. In fact, he was manning controls and jumped aboard when it appeared. What he did during this operation supposedly changed things for the next two thousand years. The project was subsequently hidden and the key vehicle (time machine) was placed in a warehouse at the Naval Air Station in Norfolk. According to this story, the right man will eventually find it.

Like Helga Morrow, the triplets have an interesting story about their birth. Baby B was a normal birth, but she was a singular baby. In a strange experiment, Baby A and Baby C were created from laboratory DNA that was alien in nature. They were accordingly amalgamated with Baby B and were born as triplets.

I have spoken to both Baby A and Baby C on the phone rather extensively. Baby A is "out there". She is quite psychic and often talks in a stream of consciousness that can be hard to follow. People take to her readily and her personal charisma has made her a remarkably popular bartender. She can naturally pack a place with people. Ironically, she'll send the majority of them to a spiritual church or other metaphysical endeavor. I also found it interesting that she knew about the incidents (mentioned in this book) concerning Duncan on Mars without me having to tell her.

Baby C is the more practical one. She is a writer and good communicator and is psychicly sensitive as well. The triplets are intimately connected and they experience frequent psychic phenomena. For example, they "tunnel" to each others rooms from across the country. In other words, they appear to each other and can communicate. According to studies, this type of phenomena is not unusual for twins. Triplets add a whole dimension to this, and I'm not yet aware of any studies that focus particularly on threes as opposed to twos.

The triplets have two other sisters plus a brother who we will refer to as "Brother". He was struck by the passage in *The Montauk Project* where Preston remembered lost time while constructing the Delta-T antenna. Both Brother and the father had similar experiences. Brother lived two lives apparently because he would go to work from a rural area, but the mileage on his car didn't add up. It showed only a few miles, yet Baby C travelled for eleven miles in every direction from his house and there was no place of work!

Brother is a machine and radio expert. He now knows that he had missing time, but he is not willing to talk at this point. Three family members in the secret service have lost their lives and there is a reticence to be known or involved in any strange projects. Once, he picked up the phone when I called Baby C. He said he knew who I was but he didn't offer any information. As Baby C talked to me, he asked his sister what she was doing. She told him that she was talking to Peter Moon. He just looked at her and said "Why?"

I invited Brother to come to Long Island, but he was afraid it might be a trap from the Government. He wanted to build some sort of protective time device first. Brother's sisters want him to open up and perhaps he will. Preston and I hope to visit the family some day.

There is another interesting story concerning this family. I was telling Baby A some information that Al Bielek had relayed to me. He had discovered that there was a complete Sage Radar (this is the same radar used at Montauk) sight at Sembach, Germany (near Nuremburg) that was fully operational. The man who told Al about this had been there for two weeks and noted that people arriving acted strangely. It was considered a mind control project.

Upon telling Baby A about this, she mentioned that her son had been stationed there. I thought this was an odd coincidence, but she was matter of fact. Her attitude was "what do you expect?" She said that her son had been working guard duty at that base and had heard people crying and screaming. The terror was amplified and terrified him to the point where he walked off his post in the middle of the night. This is an offense worthy of a court martial but the circumstances were so sensitive that he remained unpunished.

All of this sounds bizarre to the "normal" point of view, but this family takes the entire subject of Montauk and time travel with great seriousness. The triplets' father was obviously a strong influence in regards to how they look at all this. He was extremely confident and treated the intelligence and military community with irreverence. He could get away with it because his technical expertise was needed. Reportedly, trench coated personnel would come to the door and threaten and he would thumb his nose and laugh. Perhaps this behavior has something to do with his own identity. Baby A's father told her that he was an alien who just looked like a human!

25

THE INVESTIGATION CONTINUES

Montauk Point is a very cold place during the winter and most people wouldn't even consider taking a trip out there. Preston and I are no different, but we were persuaded to pay a visit and show a Hollywood producer around the base for a prospective documentary on the project. His name is Peter Beltz.

The three of us scouted out the base during the weekend before Christmas, 1992. We showed Peter the transmitter building, but it was tightly secured and still inaccessible. It was noted however that coaxial cable had been wired from the radar reflector down the sides of the structure. Preston explained that the only logical explanation for that would be to ground the reflector for lightning strikes. Apparently, there would be no reason to do that unless there were workers in the underground. We also noted that almost every building on the base had been forcibly opened and vandalized. These same structures had been locked or otherwise secured on my visit earlier that summer.

Peter was struck by the haunted atmosphere of the

place. Having also met with Duncan, he knew he had a real story on his hands and said he would return after New Year's with a camera crew. He went back to California, and we coordinated by phone how the documentary would be done. It now became necessary for me to visit Montauk and make arrangements for accomodations and an interviewing space. I went there alone and searched out the few places that were open during the off season. The trip was noteworthy for one reason. I stopped in and asked directions at a local realtor's and met Carol Brady. She was very friendly, and I told her what I was up to. Carol hadn't heard about the book, but she had some interesting stories to tell me. She said the radar reflector was still in use and that she saw it turning from time to time. Remarkably, she also said she'd witnessed a stealth aircraft actually hovering over the cliffs near the base and making absolutely no noise. This is an oddity and suggests an anti-gravity drive in the stealth.

I eventually introduced her to Preston. As she showed us pictures of her sons, Preston pointed to the oldest and said that he would be very careful regarding him because he looks just like the type the Montauk crew is after (he is blue eyed and blond haired). Carol said she was well aware to be careful. Kidnapping of blue eyed and blond haired kids was occurring as late as 1988 and the police had been very concerned and watchful. I have since found out from other sources that there is a considerable amount of crime at Montauk that is covered up as far as press coverage is concerned. Montauk is a tourist town and shocking news does not make for more people and good business.

When Peter Beltz and the camera crew arrived, we were all surprised to see that there was now a hole in the transmitter building and it was mysteriously accessible for the first time in over a year. Torch marks could be seen as

Preston described in the first book. There was also a strange device that was said to have held a giant crystal. Additionally, the name of the company that Preston worked for could be easily seen on the transmitter computer.

Perhaps the biggest find during this period was a house next to the officers' lounge. The upstairs contained the oddest "military" decor you've ever seen. One room was loud paisley, another tiger striped, and one was painted like confetti. There was a fourth room that was painted black and white in the strangest pattern arrangement. I first speculated that it might have been a base whorehouse. Preston had seen pictures of similar rooms used by the Government during the Timothy Leary (allegedly CIA financed) experiments of the 1960's. He concluded this was a programming room, and I think he is accurate. This is also some of the hardest evidence existing that irregular activity occurred at Montauk. He has it recorded and it can be viewed on his video "The Montauk Tour".

As the documentary actually got underway, the base was used as a backdrop. Duncan, Preston and Al Bielek were all interviewed separately. Preston was asked questions with the transmitter building in the background as that is where he worked. As the camera rolled, Duncan and I huddled up against a wall. It was incredibly cold. We could hear Preston describing that the Delta T antenna was below ground and that there was a null point between that and the transmitter. This is where Duncan would sit in the Montauk Chair. At the exact instant Preston described this, Duncan had a sudden and violent jolt go through his body. He went into some sort of shock state, and I placed my hand on his foot until he returned. The camera was busy on Preston and none of that incident was captured.

The entire video crew was remarkably undisturbed

during the entire shooting sequences save for a black military helicopter that circled the base on two separate occasions.

After the base footage was shot, everyone returned to a rented condo where further interviewing would be done in front of a fireplace. After hours of taping, we all broke for dinner. Someone looked out on the balcony and noticed a strange hue surrounding the Montauk base. It was faint but definitely visible and confined to the area of the base. The camera crew tried to tape it, but the hue wouldn't show on video. They did see it though. Up to this point, the phenomena with the hue has only been understandable if Duncan's readings are taken into account.

Before the documentary shooting began, Duncan's readings said it must all be completed before the 18th of January (1993) or there would be danger. His information was very specific. Further readings indicated that four aliens from the Andromedan galaxy had entered the underground base and caused some sort of etheric distortion in the electromagnetic field over Montauk. They apparently caused an explosion in the entire underground and caused untold damage to the current Montauk operation. The Andromedans are believed to be benevolent and were willing to sacrifice their lives to sabotage the Montauk underground.

This is strange information, but Preston received three phone calls indicating that something strange had occurred during this period. One friend not far from the area reported a tremor and another reported a rumbling. A third person said at least two Montauk policemen heard a big loud rumble at the base with smoke and steam coming from the buildings. Whatever the case is with these reports, security suddenly stepped up after January 18th.

On January 22nd, Preston visited the base and was

surprised to see two young women in combat fatigues strolling through the base. He politely said hello and mentioned that it was a good day for a walk. They were not friendly to say the least. Later that day, a state trooper started to arrest two civilians who happened to be strolling on the base. We thought this was extremely aggressive behavior for keeping people off a derelict base in the middle of winter. After much persuasion, he opted to give the civilians citations for trespassing. Strangely, the same officer accosted Preston but did not ticket him. He suggested that Preston could be arrested, but Preston told him that could be useful (in terms of publicity). The officer demurred and asked him to leave by the nearest exit possible.

Preston returned to the vicinity of the base a few days later and continued to shoot footage in an area outside of the base proper. Even though he was not on the base itself, the same officer (accompanied by a second officer) discovered him. Preston pointed out that he was not on forbidden territory. The second officer said they'd had enough and would harass anybody who even came close to the base. They claimed they were cracking down on vandalism. This doesn't make sense because someone had already ransacked the base months earlier and they didn't seem to care then. Preston, Duncan, and a friend of theirs were all ticketed.* While the officers talked, Preston

---

* Preston, Duncan and their friend took this case to court and eventually won. They didn't have to pay the fines. In fact, the judge was irritated with the State of New York for not posting proper signs. It should be reiterated that Preston and company were not on the base proper when they were ticketed. The officer said in the future, he would arrest anyone who came inside the fence.

As a further note of interest, the officer said he had read *The Montauk Project* and found it to be "fun". He even went to the Montauk library and asked for books on Camp Hero but was told by the librarian that this information had been taken off the shelves a few years ago as it is now classified! He didn't have any paranormal experiences of his own to relay.

left his video camera on as it dangled from his neck and some of the above conversation was recorded.

Upon returning to Preston's vehicle, they found that someone had let the air out of the right rear tire. It is unlikely that kids did that as they would have exposed themselves to passers by. Preston was told that officers sometimes used this trick to trip up anyone who is trying to get away. This not an accusation but is merely recorded as an actual occurence.

Security was now tight and it was speculated that the underground had been dismantled by the Andromedans and that the Montauk crew (including the New York state troopers) were rabidly trying to figure out what had gone wrong. Fortunately, the documentary footage was shot without any interference. Duncan's reading to get everything done before January 18th had proven very valuable.

THE MONTAUK MANOR

A tasteful and beautiful facility, the Montauk Manor consists
of condominium apartments which are rented out on a daily
basis. It is built on a Native American burial ground
and the fourth floor is said to be haunted.

26

HAUNTINGS AT MONTAUK

Had there been no interest in doing a documentary, it is questionable whether I would have travelled to Montauk at all. I had avoided the place since my visit with Maria Fix and there was no strong desire to return. The events of January 1993 had a big impact on us and there were several return trips.

Carol Brady connected us up to a local gentleman who showed us about the town and shared some interesting information with Preston and myself. He said that he'd always been fascinated by Montauk because if anyone ever wanted to conduct a clandestine activity, it would be the ideal place. The entire area is loaded with rolling hills, gullies and woods. One location can be entirely diverse from another, almost as if you had just entered another country.

This gentleman also told us that UFO sightings were not uncommon to the Montauk fishermen. Green lights and what not were often seen over the boats at sea. He pointed out that many of the fishermen are illegal aliens from Ireland and want no part of any publicity.

We then learned about the Montauk Manor. This is a huge facility that has been broken up into condos that are rentable on a daily basis. It is refurbished and has a grand ambiance. Although some locals try to keep it quiet for business reasons, there are persistent rumors that the fourth floor of the manor is haunted. The entire location is on the site of an ancient Native American burial ground which makes it a good candidate for hauntings. Perhaps the most convincing evidence of that is the story of a respected local sea captain who owned a condo in the manor. He was in his dwelling and was suddenly thrust across the room by a strong energy field. Afraid for his family, he moved them completely away from the Montauk area.

In an interesting side note, the local gentleman from Montauk also confirmed a rumor heard months earlier. Preston was getting gas at a station near Montauk and asked the young man working there if he'd heard anything strange about the old Montauk base. The young man said he'd heard that a coven of witches meets on the grounds from time to time. I did a little bit of research into this to see what I could find out. The only thing I did find out was that there are many covens on Long Island. The further east you go, the more there are and the more serious they are. The local gentleman wasn't an expert on covens, but he did say he knew a witch (a white one) who did rituals on the base. Although it is possible that she may be just one of many, we have yet to meet her or any others up to this point.

For those of you who are not familiar with witches, it should be noted that they have always centered their major activity around ley lines (energy grid points). Montauk has long been considered to be a hot bed of activity for this sort of thing.

27

NAZI GOLD

It was mentioned in *The Montauk Project* that the entire operation was possibly financed through Nazi gold that found its way to Montauk after mysteriously disappearing from an allied troop train in Strausborg, France.

I was surprised to receive an anonymous newspaper article in the mail one day that indicated that there well could have been Nazi gold used to finance the Montauk Project. But before I elaborate on that, it is time to reveal a new character in the Montauk psychodrama. His name is Kenn Arthur.

I mentioned earlier that I met Preston, Duncan and Al Bielek all on the same evening. Kenn was also there, but he seemed out of place. Intuitively, I could immediately see that he served in the Navy, and he confirmed that. He had came to the Long Island Psychotronics Chapter to buy one of Preston's psychotronic devices. I subsequently studied with him in another group, and he warned me point blank to stay away from the Psychotronics crowd. It was too dangerous. Kenn liked Preston and Duncan but it came to a point where he could no longer be around them. He thereafter has avoided the group like the plague.

As the months went by, I got to know Kenn well. I

refer to him as a walking oracle because he relays esoteric information in the most ornamented and interesting fashion. He is a personal friend of Edgar Cayce's family and studied at the A.R.E. (Association for Research and Enlightenment) for years.

Kenn was extremely cynical about Preston's story and would sometimes make up the most hysterical jokes about it. However, he would be the first to admit that he is obsessed with pessimism about anything. As time went by, I would make little discoveries that indicated that a project really did exist. He'd laugh it off in one way or another. Then, I told him about a video I saw that showed a radio device in the Montauk underground. It contained a coil wrapped around a large crystal. He didn't comment on the crystal but said everyone knew about the Montauk underground. In fact, he used to buy radar equipment from the underground when he served in the Navy. He later told me details that indicated he had served in a top secret position.

I found this all very odd. He apparently had some connection to Montauk, but he wouldn't talk about it. As time went by, the main thrust of his communication was that Preston's story was an elaborate hallucination. He said that the true story is far more bizarre than anything Preston could possibly put together. He did acknowledge that Preston sincerely believed his own story.

Preston was amused by all of this and said it confirmed that Kenn had a connection to Montauk. But we were both frustrated. If Preston's story isn't the real one, what is? He could at least have the courtesy of telling us!

Then one day I received the newspaper article in the mail that I referred to earlier. It was entitled "Hunt for Nazi Booty" and was from *The East Hampton Star* of November 14, 1985. The article tells how New York State employed a treasure hunter by the name of Ovid Arnold of Varina (should actually be Fuquay-Varina), North Carolina to use a pendulum to detect precious metal located at Camp Hero (the Montauk base). The Nazis were believed to have buried at least $12 million in cash, diamonds and gold in 1945.

Under the watchful eye of the State Park Police, an eight foot deep hole was dug where Mr. Arnold thought the treasure was buried. Officials from the state capital in Albany filmed and tape recorded the entire event.

Tom Tubbs, a spokesman for the Division of Land Utilization of the State Office of General Services was quoted as saying news of the dig was "leakproof, hush-hush to the point we didn't tell anyone why they were going to be there".

He also said the belief in the existence of the treasure was based on an old tale from 1945. According to the article, Tubbs relayed the following information.

"In 1945, the Nazis, convinced the Third Reich was about to fall, sent a U-boat to Montauk containing riches seized during the invasion of France with instructions to bury them underground inside twelve metal shell casings. The Germans sailors followed orders and buried the treasure at Camp Hero, with a large rock nearby to be used as a landmark. After the war, the money and jewels were to be used for bribes, false passports and safe passage to the United States and South America for high officers of the Reich."

According to the article, the submarine was sunk but several German sailors survived and told their story years later to the treasure hunters who wrote to the Governor and obtained permission for the hunt. The entire booty was to be split between the State and the treasure hunters. Although the treasure hunters were unsuccessful on the

November 6th dig, they wanted to return in the spring.

The entire article could well be disinformation to cover up a very successful dig. It is also possible the dowser was used by the State so that they, or some other agency, could follow through on the initial dowsing and then find the actual treasure. There were certainly more technologically sophisticated devices than dowsers for finding lost treasure in 1985. It is also thought the amount, which was quite huge at the time, was far greater.

I asked *The East Hampton Star* for permission to reprint the entire article in this book. They knew about *The Montauk Project* book and expressly refused permission to reprint.

I faxed the entire article to Kenn Arthur and was surprised by his response. He said that I was finally getting close to the actual truth of what went on there. Again, he emphasized that it was more bizarre than I could ever imagine. He told me that the German sub captain came ashore and met with the U.S. military authorities. A deal was cut with the military personnel, but the sub captain would have to go back for four additional runs and transfer more money.

Kenn believed only one run was made. The captain and other German sailors made their way ashore and settled on Long Island. He said many ended up owning barber shops on Myrtle Avenue in Ridgewood, Queens. Kenn also said he knew the families well and grew up with the captain's family. He couldn't reveal any names but said they were very respectable people.

If one looks in various books covering that time period, different mentions are made of that incident and another one where four Nazis reportedly landed in 1942 and turned themselves in after taking the Long Island Railroad to Manhattan. Most of the accounts are sketchy and offer contrary views. The incidents were filled with suspicion including complicity of J. Edgar Hoover and other top military and government officials. Some also believe that the entire operation was pulled off by the Thule Society of Germany. They engineered Hitler's rise to power and were a splinter group that derived from the Ordo Novi Templi which in turn had derived itself from the Ordo Templi Orientis* which was associated with Aleister Crowley. For some reason, no matter which way we turn, this man keeps coming back into the picture.

* This information is according to THE OCCULT CONSPIRACY, Secret Societies – Their Influence and Power in World History by Michael Howard, Destiny Books, One Park Street, Rochester, Vermont, 05767. It should also be noted that the practices and principles of the above organizations are not considered to be in alignment with those of the O.T.O.

THE MONTAUK TOWER

Construction on the Montauk Tower began in about the 1920's,
but the work was not completed for decades.
Over the years it has been nearly impossible to find tenants
or a suitable purpose for the building. Of interest to our story is that
the catacombs of Montauk supposedly lead to this tower
which is located in downtown Montauk.

28

CATACOMBS OF MONTAUK

The next point of intrigue concerning Montauk came when I received a phone call from David Adair, the president of Sirius Minds* in New York City. He had spent New Year's Eve at the Montauk Manor just after reading *The Montauk Project: Experiments in Time*. While speaking with one of the managers of the estate, he was told about tunnels underneath the grounds that were referred to as the catacombs. The manager took him to the basement and showed David where many of the entry ways had been sealed with cinderblock. There were various crawl spaces that were accessible but all of this was more than he could explore in a short outing.

Upon hearing from David, I gave Preston a call and asked him about the catacombs. He was nonchalant about the subject and said he'd known about them for years. They were not of much interest to him. He told me that according to legend, they were connected to the Montauk base.

I called Kenn Arthur and told him about the catacombs. He again said I was getting closer to what was really going

---

* Sirius Minds is a psychotronic salon which is sometimes referred to as a brain gymnasium. This company works with corporate clients or individuals to enhance brain capacity and enhance life functions.

on. According to Kenn, the catacombs are a pathway to the Inner Earth. He spoke about the catacombs of Rome and a few other places. According to legend, there are many such entry ways. Also included would be the labyrinth of Crete, the Incan tunnels in the Andes and the underground passages used by the Viet Cong.

The next day, Preston was at my house and overheard me talking on the phone to someone about the catacombs possibly leading to the Inner Earth. He became very interested in that possibility. Then he came out with what I call "vintage Preston". He spieled off a load of information about the catacombs that he probably didn't even have access to ten minutes before. He said that the catacombs were built during the early part of this century, probably in the teens. The Kaiser of Germany had a multitude of spies and sympathizers on Long Island and had financed many of them. The Kaiser had his own purposes in mind. Preston also said the catacombs lead to the Montauk Tower in downtown Montauk and travel all the way to the base and down along the shore through an area called Ditch Plains.

Preston humorously recalled going to Mark Hamill's (or the person thought to be Mark Hamill) mansion and discovering the underground tunnels which were connected right to the mansion. Dick Cavett was in the mansion next door and Preston said the tunnel connected to Cavett's house as well. He said they used to sneak in on occasion and mysteriously rearrange the furniture in the living room.

Al Bielek was not so amused when I told him about the catacombs. He remembered some aspects of them from the Montauk base, but didn't know how extensive they were. He felt that Preston had been withholding the information from him. It also explained to him how

188

Preston was able to acquire so much of the underground equipment. Al had recognized some of Preston's equipment from the Montauk underground but could never figure out how he had managed to get at it. The catacombs were the obvious answer.

I explained that Preston probably just didn't remember it. He's funny that way. On some days he'll suddenly remember a vast amount of information that he could have been totally oblivious to the day before. It is interesting to note that it was the suggestion of the Inner Earth which triggered his recall.

There is another aspect to the catacombs which may involve Aleister Crowley. The German Kaiser was mentioned previously and there is no question that Crowley was a supporter of his, at least verbally. He was hired in the United States to write propaganda for the German cause during World War I and someone in the British government even tried to convict him of treason. Crowley escaped any trouble by claiming he was working for British intelligence. Whatever the truth is, Crowley was a very influential person and could have been playing both sides of the coin for magical purposes. This entire relationship with the Kaiser makes Crowley's visit to Montauk all the more intriguing.

Crowley also had a friend on Long Island by the name of Otto Kahn. Kahn was a famous financier and incredibly influential himself. In 1917, he chose the highest point on Long Island on which to build his mansion. It still exists today but visitors are not encouraged. There have been persistent rumors about underground tunnels that lead to and from the mansion. One of these was supposed to lead to Manhattan.

I circulated this story at an evening discussion on Montauk and one of the people in the audience had a strong interest in Otto Kahn and his mansion. He said that he used to visit there on bike rides but that access was almost entirely cut off. He said that the mansion was turned into a boys military academy and was eventually closed down. He backed this up by sending me articles from *Newsday*, Long Island's daily newspaper, that indicated the school was closed in 1978 as "unsafe and unfit for human habitation". There were scores of fire violations with students crammed into small, sometimes windowless rooms. Garbage and cockroaches were on the floor, all in the presence of exposed wiring. Further, the toilets were frequently not working with excrement spilling onto the floors.

This entire scenario is the spitting image of what has been described at Montauk for the boys program. There was total and complete disregard of humane factors which is the total opposite of what you would expect at a military academy.

It could be a meaningless coincidence that this school reached its nadir while the Montauk Project was in full swing. But the intriguing connection to Crowley and the tunnels warrant that it be mentioned. It is hoped with this that we will hear from cadets who actually attended the school.

29

MADAME X

What you have just read completes the more tangible aspects of the Montauk investigation up to this point. What we are about to embark on now is considerably more abstract and speculative, but the synchronicity in the circumstances you are about to read is undeniable. The information is in line with certain esoteric doctrines and will be old hat to some readers. For those who are not familiar, I will try to make it as understandable as possible.

All of this concerns a chance meeting I had with a woman I will refer to as Madame X. Long before *The Montauk Project* was published, she had come to Long Island to visit the Montauk base. Afterwards, she visited with Preston, myself and a few others. I was struck by her immense knowledge and understanding and spoke to her afterwards. A year after our first meeting, we began to talk on a regular basis.

I was very surprised to hear from her that she had known about the situation at Montauk long before Preston had gone public with his story. She knew highly personalized information about Duncan which came from an entirely independent source. Madame X explained to me that certain mystery schools have had a very strong interest in Duncan for a long time. He is a heavily watched and monitored individual.

After a while, Madame X began to reveal information to me on a fairly steady basis. She explained that there are twelve major mystery schools on planet Earth and that she seeks to monitor their various activities. Instinctively a rebel, she is not a member of any of them. Although her position is extremely unique, it fits the esoteric tradition perfectly as described in Hermann Hesse's novels. Her entire family is likewise loaded with similar connections. She also explained that it is a wise precaution not to use her name as her sources of information could be cut off if it were found out what she was saying to me. The data that follows has been inspired from a year's worth of conversations with her.

What is a mystery school?

Also known as secret societies, these are organized groups that have been around since time immemorial. Their names sometimes change with the winds of politics but throughout history there have been many branches. The Illuminati, Knights Templars, Masons and Rosicrucians are just a few samples of organizations that have been identified as mystery schools. While the aforesaid are well known throughout history and are at times considered notorious, there are others that work more secretly in an effort to balance what the others have done. The Order of Melchizedek, the Magi and the Order of the Seven Rays would all fit into the latter category. I don't know the full organizational charts and interrelationships of all the groups. That is a job for conspiracy theorists. At this point, we are concerned with the mystery schools as a whole and not one specific organization.

All of these societies have their own agendas. They can be dangerous or noble, depending on the nature of the people operating in the various schools. Modern society would appear to be regulated by them in the most mysterious ways. They could also be considered the gatekeepers of knowledge. Madame X tries to monitor the information and activities of the different secret societies and relay whatever communications she can to promote universal balance; hence, her involvement with Montauk.

Since the beginning, the twelve major mystery schools have been concerned with the balance of good and evil or light and dark. It is in this realm with which we can identify the Antichrist. The Antichrist is important because it is the focal point of what Montauk is about. Not only was Duncan trained in this tradition but Crowley used "The Beast" as his logo.

The common reaction to the concept of an Antichrist is that it is evil and to be avoided at all costs. It is not quite that simple. Philosophically and empirically, if there is a Christ, it would stand to reason that there is an Antichrist. This is reflective of the common duality upon which the universe is based such as yin-yang, etc. Christ is, of course, perceived as good. However, the equation becomes complicated when there is an imbalance between the two. For example, the Inquisition championed the name of Christ and committed some of the worst atrocities in history. The very concept of Christ became polluted and was the mouthpiece for the forces of darkness.

During this period in history, certain mystery schools began to actively promote pagan rites in the name of Baphomet or Mephistopheles which equates to the Antichrist. The goal of this was to magically reverse the polarity of the Catholic Church. The Church denied and squashed the beast in man, but the pagans promoted it. Man is a spirit but his body is resonant to the world of beasts. To deny this relationship creates an imbalance which results in all sorts of ills upon the world.

On a more broad scale, an imbalance of either the Christ or Antichrist creates a disharmony in the continuum of life. The trick to all of this is balancing the two polarities so as not to get lost in either direction. Achieving this harmony could be called "the middle way", the Tao or the manifestation of the Holy Spirit. It depends upon what belief system you subscribe to.

Crowley, of course, identified with the Beast because it reversed the evils that had been perpetrated upon him in the name of "Christ". This is simply a magical formula and has no reference to good or bad. In order to understand the full nature of such a formula, one should consult Crowley's various books on Magick. It should be pointed out that Crowley was a human being who errored and committed both good and bad deeds. More important, and beyond judgement of good and evil, he was a magician. In that role, he was also ultimately concerned with balancing forces and releasing the universe from untold torments.

To Crowley, raising the Antichrist did not mean summoning the devil. It meant balancing energies that had gone off the rails. For example, if a person was ill from sexual repression, kissed a crucifix every night and associated their illness/repression with Christ, a dance with the devil just might restore their health. This has more to do with semantics and subconscious associations than good or evil. And don't forget that Jesus acted nasty and outrageous when He kicked the money changers out of the temple. It was the right action for the moment.

Of further intrigue in all this is another esoteric doctrine. And that is that the balance of the Christ and Antichrist has everything to do with our own entrapment in time. These energies run rampantly through us on a daily basis. Sometimes you might want to help somebody out of the charity of your heart. Other times you might want to give someone a whack. Knowing what to do and when to do it is the key. Charity to a terrorist could have dire consequences for everyone. When these energies flow in a union of balance, harmony is achieved. One rises above duality and attains Christ Consciousness which is outside of space and time as we commonly know it. An example of this can be seen with Buddha sitting under the Bodhi tree. He confronted completely the desire to do good and the desire to do evil. He was tethered to neither but promoted the balance of all forces.

Crowley defined yoga as meaning union and sin as restriction. These definitions by themselves can be very useful on an every day practical basis. In a magical ceremony, Crowley or someone else might raise the Antichrist for the purpose of lifting the restriction that has already impaled one on the cross of space and time (the cross, by the way, has long been a symbol of space and time).

Many ceremonies, masses and what not have been authored throughout the centuries to promote the facility of leaving this dimension. While some might be quite comical, others are infinitely elaborate and based upon the most carefully guarded secrets in the universe. The success of such an operation depends on who is doing it and why. But the basic theory of any ceremony should recognize that the universe is based upon polarity or two dimensions. A ninety degree shift from a two dimensional universe (such as Christ-Antichrist, yin-yang, etc.) would be necessary to enter the third dimension. Likewise, another ninety degree shift would be necessary to enter the fourth dimension. This is not easy to visualize, but if you can, you are likely to protract your consciousness right into the fourth dimension.

Once you have ascended into the fourth dimension, you are fully conscious of the relativity of time. It is from this realm (including higher dimensions than the fourth) that manipulation of time can occur. It is also from this realm that infinite healing and enlightenment can begin. If one has ascended into higher dimensions, the relative truth of the Philadelphia Experiment and Montauk Project won't matter. They could be changed and rearranged and rescripted. The purpose of this book and of our promulgating the Montauk legend is to raise consciousness of higher planes in hopes that we may ascend.

Duncan was trained to be a factor in a grand experiment. That it failed is quite obvious. At Montauk, the Antichrist factors took over to the point where evil ran wild. If we believe Stan Campbell's information, Christ Himself played the magician by turning the tables and balancing out the evil factors. Whatever magicians do, these forces will naturally ebb and flow throughout the universe on their own. But there is no reason a magician or a certain society can't be a catalyst for such forces. In the next chapter, we will examine a very ambitious attempt to harness the forces of nature and thereby change the universe and the interdimensional relationships therein.

30

THE BABALON WORKING

In 1946, one of the most celebrated and significant magical experiments of the century occurred. It was called the Babalon Working. The participants were some of the most colorful characters in recent history: Jack Parsons, Cameron and L. Ron Hubbard.

When I first became involved in the Montauk investigation, I had no idea that I would be led to Marjorie Cameron. I had always been interested in what had gone on between Hubbard and Parsons, but I didn't know about Cameron and never would have looked her up if it had not been for my fascination with the synchronicity between the Camerons and the Crowleys. That her real name was Wilson was quite astounding, but even so, I have had a hard time admitting that she could have anything to do with the Montauk story. It seemed either too corny or too good to be true. Madame X has pushed my nose into this and has finally gotten me to see that the synchronicity of my meeting Cameron (under the odd circumstances that I did) was not an accident. After all, I have now personally met two of the principals in the Babalon Working. Unfortunately, Jack Parsons died before I was born. He is definitely the most enigmatic of the three. An important and intriguing figure when it comes to the subject of interdimensional shifts, Parsons appears in countless footnotes by many different authors. His life was a labyrinth of mystery and his writings are difficult to find. We will examine key parts of his life and then look at his involvement in the Babalon Working before we come full circle back to Montauk.

Parsons was born into a wealthy Pasadena family in 1914. Although he attended the University of Southern California, he was apparently too brilliant to stay in college. He had a remarkable reputation as an explosives expert and as said previously in this book, he was a principal scientist with the rocket research group attached to Cal Tech that founded the Jet Propulsion Laboratory.

If it takes a rocket scientist to understand magick, Jack Parsons was certainly a fast and furious student of the subject. He was introduced to the O.T.O. by a scientist friend and was particularly impressed by the fact that Crowley had predicted the work of Einstein and the quantum theory in his book *Liber Legis*.

Jack joined the O.T.O. in 1941 and at one point served as Lodge Master for the Agapé Lodge of the order. He became associated with L. Ron Hubbard after the war ended and together they participated in the "Babalon Working" with Marjorie Cameron, Jack's second wife. The Babalon Working was a magical ritual that lasted days and is probably the most famous magical working of the 20th century. An entire book could and should be written about the Babalon Working. In this chapter, we will give only a brief summary of what happened.

Parsons was considered by some to be the spiritual heir of Aleister Crowley, but this magical working would set Parsons' life on a new path and lead to the end of his relationship with Crowley and L. Ron Hubbard. It involved creating a Moonchild which was the raising of the Antichrist as was explained in the last chapter. Parsons also viewed this experiment as reversing the stagnant and unbalanced patriarchal power structure of the Piscean era. He was also a big fan of womankind and in this work he sought to bring out the Goddess energy that had been repressed for millennia.

What exactly is a Moonchild? There are differing views. Cameron explained to me that she's uncomfortable with the word. She said that every time one has sex, a thought form is created. This is sometimes called a Moonchild. The thought form will go out and do the bidding of the magicians involved (sex partners).

A Moonchild is also considered to be the Antichrist by some, but there is an interesting polarity in the word. The moon is reflective and acts as a shadow. The sun, which is mythologically referenced to be in alignment with Lucifer, is considered to have opposite polarity to the moon. This gives the moon a redemptive quality. On the other hand, the moon can also be associated with darkness and sorcery. Again, it is all a manner of semantics and what style of forces the magician chooses to invoke.

The Babalon Working began in 1946 with a full ritual ceremony. Parsons and Cameron gave their sexual energy with Hubbard overseeing the operation and using his astral vision. It was an exhaustive operation which was designed to open an interdimensional door for the manifestation of the goddess Babalon (which means understanding), the Mother of the Universe. She would appear in human form, and many to this day consider that Cameron is indeed the incarnation of Babalon. I agree that Cameron is a very impressive and magnetic character, and I would never deny that she is Babalon but it is not my job to pass judgment. But I do not think she was intended to be a Moonchild. That is something else. In fact, she feels that many of the children born in the 1960's. are "her children" in a magical sense. The Moonchild has been considered by some to be the spiritual heir to Crowley. As Cameron and Parsons had no children, the Moonchild should be relegated to a birth in a different dimension (which could well have infiltrated this world in almost any form).

Much to Parsons' surprise, Crowley did not take kindly to his experiment. He sent someone to effectively take over and muster Jack out of the O.T.O. According to what Hymenaeus Beta (the Outer Head of the O.T.O.) told me, Parsons was experimenting in forces that he could not control and would lead to trouble.

So what did Jack Parsons actually do?

According to the accounts of many others, Parsons (along with Hubbard and Cameron) succeeded in creating a rift in space-time (not unlike the Philadelphia Experiment). A doorway to "the other side" or another dimension was created. It was after this operation that UFO sightings began to be reported en masse. The famous Roswell crash occurred in 1947, prior to the death of Aleister Crowley. Whatever happened during the Babalon Working, there is extremely wide acceptance in both magical and scientific circles that something of an extremely profound nature occurred that had an extreme interdimensional effect. Besides the massive UFO sightings that followed, there was also the National Security Act and the formation of the CIA.

It is also noteworthy to point out that according to Cameron, both Parsons and Hubbard were never the same after the experiment. Both would have many struggles and Parsons would be officially assassinated six years later. Ironically, the Capitol building in Washington, D.C. was stormed by UFOs within a very short time after Parsons died.

At this point, we are invited to speculate about the Babalon Working. It was most definitely a magical act which was aspiring to reach the realm of creation (God) itself. If the creation zone were accessed, history could have been rewritten or changed by the very power of God or lesser minions. Most would never know the difference. Based upon the above information, mistakes were made during the operation. This leaves a trail we can follow.

If Jack Parsons was a failure in his efforts, it would appear to be as a result of infiltration from another dimension. (The violation of women through alien abductions is a somewhat related example.) He opened himself up to an alien force which has gotten the better of many of us. Perhaps this is what Crowley was so concerned about when he kicked Parsons out of the O.T.O. In any case, Parsons was a pioneer in an area that is only now becoming popular. He was a maverick and a radical and that is what brings about changes and progress. Hopefully, we can learn from this man's errors.

The Babalon Working not only opened the door to interdimensionality, it sought to create a spiritual heir to Crowley. While Cameron could well be that heir, there are other possibilities as well. We will address that a little bit later.

The next question to consider is: how does all this relate to Montauk?

DELTA T ANTENNA

This is an actual Delta T antenna that sits above Space Time Labs
on Long Island. By definition, it can actually facilitate
shifting time zones. Two coils are placed vertically around the edges of
the pyramid structure at ninety degree angles to one another.
A third coil surrounds the base. Shifting time zones was
accomplished by pulsing and powering the antenna,
as is discussed in *The Montauk Project: Experiments in Time*.
Even when the antenna is not powered,
it has a subtle interdimensional effect
on the nature of time itself.

31

CROWLEY CHRONICLE

As I alluded to earlier, until now I had been resistant to seeing a clear connection between Montauk, Cameron and the Babalon Working. At Madame X's suggestion, I reviewed my experiences on the whole matter. I will now share with you the various factors of how Crowley came into my life.

My first encounter with witchcraft was as a high school student. I was reading some book that was totally lambasting witches and the supernatural. It was so prejudiced that I began to wonder about the subject in general. Almost every book on the subject in our library treated the subject with extreme scorn or laughter. It absolutely couldn't be taken seriously. There was so much prejudice that I figured there must be something to the subject. That began my interest in the paranormal. I did find a book by Sybil Leek that was instructive. She explained the Old Religion and said witches were a misnomer for the ancient Druid priests and priestesses. She mentioned a man by the name of Aleister Crowley who was a relative and used to read poetry to her in the mountains. Sybil made a point of saying he wasn't the wicked man everyone thought. That was my first recognition of Crowley.

My next experience had to do with Monique Wilson. During my research into the Cameron-Wilson connection, I discovered that she was from Scotland and was considered the "Queen of the Witches". She created much controversy in the witch world in the 1970's when she sold her rightfully inherited witch memorabilia to *Ripley's Believe It or Not* museum. Some thought it was too commercial and denigrated witchcraft as an art, but if it were not for this act, I might never have had Crowley step further into my life.

In 1974, I was stationed on a Sea Organization (the elite management branch of Scientology) ship named *Excalibur*. We were docked at Fisherman's Wharf in San Francisco and a few of us decided to jump ship and look for something to do after 11:00 P.M. There isn't much to do around there that late at night, so we tried to go to the Ripley museum. It had just closed, but they told us the witchcraft museum next door (it has since moved or closed down) was open. My friends and I went in and had a good many laughs. The museum was very hokey. But the biggest laugh of all was when we came to a waxed figure of Aleister Crowley, "The Wickedest Man in the World". He was brandishing a knife over a naked lady and looked quite mad. My friends and I laughed and talked about it for months later.

Within a week, a man came aboard ship with his head shaved and looked just like Aleister Crowley. We joked that this man was the "wickedest in the world". Within six months, this man worked his way into a position of financial trust and absconded with $30,000. We wondered if Crowley had had the last laugh. Actually, the man returned to the scene of the crime within six months and another friend of mine escorted him to the police and he was immediately jailed. The whole experience was quite bizarre.

Later on, in the late 1970's, I would work for Hubbard and find that he would get letters calling him the Beast 666. I had never read the Bible up to that point and thought this was all extremely funny. The letters were never answered as they were derogatory but many jokes ensued. I was eventually told that a court case in England had cleared L. Ron Hubbard of any connection to Aleister Crowley. Although Hubbard's affection for Crowley was stated in Church authorized tapes (which I hadn't heard at the time), I wasn't aware there had been any connection and it seemed like an absurd issue.

As the 666 messages continued to come in (this was during the time Montauk was in full swing), the jokes became funnier. I even used "666" as the combination on my briefcase as it was so easy to remember. A year later, I would loan the briefcase to a friend. He asked for the combination and stood opened mouth when I told him. He told me that was his number and that he'd been a man called Aleister Crowley in a past life. I thought this was another absurd past life claim to fame, but it certainly perked my attention. He insisted that I look at one of Crowley's books. I told him it looked interesting but that I didn't have the time for it. This same man was also a friend of my wife to be and he served as my best man. He is still in the Church today and while I don't believe he is Aleister Crowley, the incident made quite an impression on me. Oddly, there are many aspects of his personality that are similar to Crowley. He did study Crowley quite profusely when he was a San Francisco hippie and this could account for his strong identification with the man. In some respects, he was also one of the most brilliant people I'd ever met, but he had some shortcomings. One was a severe case of epilepsy. I would later read in a book that Edgar Cayce considered this a symptom of having been sexually promiscuous and abusive of psychic powers in a previous life. Whatever the case with my friend, there was a very synchronous pattern at work. In hindsight, it would appear that someone or something was trying to communicate to me. The code word was Crowley.

My next encounter with Crowley came when reading a book called *L. Ron Hubbard: Messiah or Madman?* by Bent Corydon and L. Ron Hubbard, Jr. It is a discreditable book about Hubbard, and I consider it to be a severe distortion of the whole truth about the man, but the authors did me a service. Many pertinent facts were brought to light which indicated that Hubbard had studied Crowley profusely. I slowly began to read everything I could find by Aleister Crowley. It explained a lot.

There is another interesting experience about this time period. Just before or during the time I read the above book, I found myself totally outside of my body (during sleep) in the middle of space. A horrible looking hag of a witch was looking at me. She was utterly hideous and had some sort of direct line to me. I simply confronted her and looked her straight in the eye. Her face slowly faded to reveal a bust of Hubbard. It crumbled into dust and fell away. I woke up and felt like a spell had been broken. On a subjective basis, this coincided with my discovery of Crowley's influence on Scientology. None of this is to say that Hubbard was practicing witchcraft or black magic, but the experience is interesting to note.

As time went by, I became very knowledgeable about Aleister Crowley and his writings, but I never joined any groups or became a ceremonial magician. Off and on, I studied these materials for about four years. All this information I'd accumulated was apparently just waiting to be accessed. The grand design was at work.

My next episode with Crowley was meeting Preston

Nichols. I'd met him briefly just before a lecture. He said we could talk afterwards. There was a break in the middle, and I remember asking him a question. I don't remember exactly what it was, but the first thing he mentioned to me was about Aleister Crowley and the Wilson brothers. This is odd as Preston hardly ever mentions this subject, let alone at lectures or to complete strangers, yet these were practically his first words to me. I hadn't mentioned Aleister Crowley. He did. It appears the universe made the connection for us.

You've since read about my encounter with Cameron and how I arrived at her doorstep. But it doesn't end there. Just before the manuscript for this book was completed, I took one last trip to the library to check the derivation of the word "Montauk". Much to my surprise, I would find three references to the name Parsons in Montauk history. The particular associations do not seem to signify anything other than a possible family connection between Jack and Montauk. This prompted me to call Cameron and inquire about Jack's family. I did find out that Jack's family were among the first settlers and shippers in Massachusetts and were very influential on the East Coast. This makes the Montauk connection all the more plausible.

Cameron also had another instance of synchronicity to report which I considered even more interesting. She mentioned that the name "Wilson" appears all over Los Angeles. She referenced Mount Wilson and said that there are several important Wilsons around town. In fact, she said that her current connection with the Jet Propulsion Laboratory was a Wilson. A Jim Wilson had contacted her in about 1991. She'd been out of touch with JPL since the 1950's and he suddenly invited her down for a tour.

Then, Cameron dropped a bomb on me. She told me

that practically her whole family (the Cameron family) had worked at JPL during Jack's tenure there. It was embarrassing to the family because Jack was a security risk. He was always under investigation by the Government and this had a tendency to put their jobs in jeopardy.

Now, it was almost forty years since Jack Parsons' death and Cameron and her grandson were mysteriously summoned to the Jet Propulsion Laboratory for a tour of the modern day facility. Jim Wilson conducted the tour which ended in the observation booth whereupon Cameron read him the introduction to Jack's book *Freedom is A Two-Edged Sword*. After she finished, she was immediately escorted out. It did not go over too big, but Wilson surprisingly confessed to being a fan of L. Ron Hubbard and said that he had read everything Hubbard wrote. Cameron would later call Jim Wilson and ask him to help her on a personal matter. After that was discussed, she asked him if he'd heard about the Montauk experiment. He became suddenly silent and hung up.

There was also another oddity about Jim Wilson. He claimed to know all about Jack Parsons. Obviously, he must have been interested or he wouldn't have called Cameron. He showed her a life size photo of the original rocket research team at Cal Tech. Although Jack's picture was there, he couldn't recognize it and pointed to Ed Forman, who he said was Jack. This is very bizarre because I know for a fact that Jim Wilson knows a lot about Jack Parsons. I have a copy of an interview he did with Dr. Frank Malina who conducted the initial rocket tests with Jack. Practically the whole interview was about Jack Parsons. This man was up to something, but Cameron gave him a jolt he wasn't expecting. It must have been the truth. Sometimes that scares people.

I relayed this information to Preston, and he made an

interesting comment. He said he wondered if Jack Pruitt (who is mentioned in the first book as Preston's boss at the Montauk Project) was indeed Jack Parsons who had gone through a witness location program. He also said that he'd been speaking with a friend at NASA who told him that years ago, the buzz around NASA was that JPL originally stood for "Jack Parsons Laboratory". The name "Jet Propulsion Laboratory" was a cover.

I told Cameron about this and she sort of snickered and said, "It fits, doesn't it?"

Of further interest was another encounter with Mr. X (mentioned in Chapter 8) who heard me talk to a small group about some of this information. I was discussing Jack Parsons and synchronicities with the name "Wilson", but I did not mention Jack Pruitt once. At the end of my talk, he said the information about Jack Pruitt was interesting. I had mentioned Jack Parsons, not Pruitt! He had subconsciously connected the two on his own, perhaps based on his own involvement at Montauk. The next day he acted suspicious and told me he had thrown that out there to see how I would react.

It is hard for me to accept that Jack Pruitt and Jack Parsons could be one and the same, but I definitely thought it possible that Jack's death could have been a smoke screen. I spoke to Cameron and asked if she'd actually seen Jack's body after he died. She said no and that she sometimes wondered if he had been taken hostage. Later, she was not too enthusiastic about the prospect because she recalled that one of the local firemen had spent a good deal of time with Jack on the day he died. He gave her a convincing report on what had happened. I find it suspicious that a fireman would spend a great deal of time with someone on the day they supposedly were killed from a pyrotechnic style explosion. After all, a captain in the New

York City Fire Department once told me that most arsonists masquerade as firemen. He said it was a statistical fact. In this case, the fireman could have been entertaining or otherwise distracting Jack while his lab was being set up to explode.

All of this experience reveals an amazing synchronicity between Jack Parsons, JPL and Montauk. In fact, it asks for an even deeper investigation that is obviously beyond the scope of this present book.

Cameron has instructed me that synchronicity is the entire basis of magick. Magick, as it has been defined by Crowley, is the entire basis of our universe. She also said that synchronicity carries forward from one life to another and that might explain some of my current research. I'm not ready to comment on any of that, but there are some things I should say about Cameron. Upon reading the initial manuscript of this book, she became cautious about being associated with the Montauk Project and distanced herself from the subject. She did say that the Montauk Project might simply be a reflection of Jack and his work. Many people have implied that Jack failed but he didn't necessarily fail at all. Cameron said the Babalon Working mandated that he must become "the fire" and he did. His success or failure cannot be determined for a least one hundred years.

Interestingly, Preston did not disagree that the entire Montauk Project could have been a magical reflection of Jack Parsons. The various synchronicities discussed still require a lot more explanation. More importantly for this work, they do indicate some sort of tie between Montauk and the Babalon Working, all via the name "Wilson". I will attempt to draw the connection full circle after we examine another candidate considered by some to be Aleister Crowley's spiritual heir.

32

CROWLEY RISING

In an earlier chapter, I mentioned that I had received a letter from Amado Crowley verifying the existence of the Wilson brothers. According to his book *The Secrets of Aleister Crowley*, his father had many children out of wedlock and he chose Amado (which means beloved) to leave his spiritual heritage to.

As to the authenticity of his parentage, there is some controversy. The O.T.O. does not consider Amado Crowley to be either an heir or a son of Aleister Crowley. Other people have verified that he is indeed the real son of Crowley but this has been on a psychic and graphology (handwriting analysis) basis. None of this is court of law proof or necessarily true otherwise. For that, we would have to exhume Aleister Crowley and do some DNA testing. I'm sure he would have relished the idea, but alas, he was cremated. (I can just see him rigging the coffin in his will so that his tongue would pop out in the event that he was exhumed.) I continued to correspond with Amado as the manuscript for *Montauk Revisited* was written, and he volunteered some very interesting additional information.

About the Babalon Working, he said that Parsons and Hubbard were censured because they were very interested

in "chaos theory". In the occult sense, they were seeking the forces that would "reverse" or "undo" the created universe with a view to harnessing them. If this is true, it seems to me that Aleister Crowley was very concerned that they might actually succeed. And if we listen to others, they certainly did!

As for the Philadelphia Experiment and how it might relate to his father, he told me that I would be intrigued to find out where Aleister Crowley was on August 12, 1943 (the day of the Philadelphia Experiment). I wrote back and told him that I'd like to know not only that but where his father was on August 12, 1923 and August 12, 1903 (this is in reference to the twenty year biorhythms of the Earth). I received a quick reply.

"On the 12th August, 1943, Aleister Crowley, myself, and five other people were gathered round an ancient stone monument, called Men-an-Tol, near Morvah in Cornwall, England. You will note the remarkable similarity of the name to Montauk. I enclose a photocopy of a postcard. The stone itself is called "a quoit" because it has a large circular hole in it. I was made to lie on a length of board, and this was inserted (me with it) into the hole. It was like the ferrite rod that is put into an electric coil. Aleister performed a ritual which appeared to "cause" a line of "rough water" between this spot in southern England, and Long Island in the USA."

It should be duly noted at this point that the O.T.O. disputes Amado's claim and has provided a quote from the typescript of Aleister Crowley's unpublished diary for August 12, 1943: "40th anniversary of my first marriage. Ill all day: damned ill. Insomnia, choked nostrils, dry mouth & throat. Yet on M.B. coming at 7:30 P.M. I woke up bit by bit & wrote well, clearly, & vigorously to Saturnus [Karl Germer of OTO], Roy [Leffingwell of

OTO], Chris Kraemer. 2.30 Insomnia; better after sleeping 4:30 A.M.—11 A.M. break for brekker [breakfast]."

At first glance, it would appear that Amado is incorrect on his dates at the very least. But it is very interesting to note that this day (assuming the O.T.O.'s typescript to be authentic) was the 40th anniversary of Crowley's marriage to Rose, the woman who directed him to write *The Book of the Law*, his most inspired work and the core of his legacy. This is at the very least a "biorhythmic synchronicity" in that it is exactly forty years before the Philadelphia Experiment. The anniversary of Crowley's wedding is very important to the O.T.O. and they honored it by having a feast on August 12, 1993.

It should also be noted that the above quote provided by the O.T.O. does not entirely preclude the possibility of Aleister Crowley being at Men-an-Tol on August 12th. In fact, just before this book went to press, I received a letter from Amado Crowley. It even arrived on August 12, 1993! I had told Amado about the discrepancy between his account and that provided by the O.T.O. I will now quote from his letter of July 26th.

"Thank you for offering me the chance to 're-think' the date when Crowley and I were in Cornwall, doing that 'human magnet' trick. There is no need for me to change a thing. It was extremely helpful of the O.T.O. to provide a copy of the entry in AC's diaries ... but, you know, I do have access to them — the originals are kept in London. So when I said we were at Men-an-Tol, you can take it for granted that I knew about the discrepancy with the diaries. I chose not to alter a thing because I am right, and the diaries are not. Never mind what he wrote. Ask rather, for whom did he write it? There are a great many other occasions when 'what Crowley wrote' seems to be at odds with 'what Crowley did'.

"Is there any mention of 'The Hess Affair'* in the diaries? Does he once mention that the French 'Deuxiéme Bureau' financed the Abbey of Thelema?** Spies are not quite as stupid as the O.T.O. seem to think. I doubt if they are even aware of the 'agents' in their own organization! But this much is certain: no spies, not even those portrayed in Hollywood films, have a habit of chatting about it openly. Instead, they do all they can to turn attention away from what they are up to. In 1943, please tell the O.T.O., we in Europe were at war too! It may be news to them, being upright and honest, but Aleister was in the habit of 'covering his tracks'."

More importantly, and long before Amado had heard about Montauk from me, he had stated that Crowley spent time in Cornwall before the end of his life. That he was able to recognize the connection between Men-an-Tol and Montauk is significant. Before I had heard from the O.T.O., I took Amado's letter to someone familiar with Gaelic linguistics. They informed me that "Men-an-Tol" and "Montauk" (which is a Native American name) come from the same root and mean the same thing. Unfortunately, both dialects are lost and you can only find conjectures in library texts. I am told both words trace back to the root "mer". This is associated with the sea but also means a circle of perpetual motion, like a vortex through which creation can manifest and from which one can conjure. The root of these words has actually turned into a separate research project and will be expounded upon at a later date. It should be noted however that all the

---

*"The Hess Affair" refers to Crowley's involvement in a plan that lured Hitler's deputy, Rudolph Hess, to parachute to Scotland. It involved a magical ritual and also routine intelligence activity.
** The Abbey of Thelema was a retreat in Sicily run by Crowley and allegedly financed by French intelligence. Mussolini, upon hearing of Crowley's occult powers, expelled him from Italy in the 1920s.

Native American shamans are reported to have worshipped spirit guides referred to as the "Manatu". These were shape shifters and time travellers according to legend, and the root of the name is related to the word "Montauk".

So, even if Amado Crowley is considered to be inaccurate on his dates, his scholarship is noteworthy. Additionally, the fact that his letter to me arrived on August 12th definitely gives him a definite degree of credibility if one recognizes the principles of synchronicity. There is, of course, considerable controversy concerning Amado and we do not wish to take an official position on his legitimacy but merely report the data that has come to us. What is important is that his information is undeniably synchronous with our own research.

Of further interest is Crowley's whereabouts on August 12, 1923. Amado says that he was "in the desert, just outside of Tunis, where he had been 'on retreat' with Leah Hirsig and Norman Mudd. As a companion, he had an Arab boy called (surprise, surprise) Mohammed. They were in the tent of an important sheik who acknowledged Crowley as a Master. It was on this occasion that they prepared the way for Crowley to become the new head of the Karl Germer branch of the OTO."

On August 12, 1903, Amado was not so sure. We now know from the O.T.O. that Crowley was married on that day. Amado said that was just after the final end of the Golden Dawn, a major magical society of which Crowley, William Butler Yeats and many notables were members. He suspected that Aleister received information on that date about locating "The Book of Desolation" which deals, among other things, with the "wiles of chaos". This opens the door to infinite possibilities. It is also noteworthy to point out that according to legend, the Wilson

217

brothers, or at least one of them, died in 1902 or 1903. According to Preston Nichols, this approximate date began the downfall of science. It became a twisted and warped subject as it fixated upon materiality to the point of excluding discoveries that were not in alignment with prescribed thought patterns.

Another intriguing aspect about "The Book of Desolation" is that it was said to be found in or near the tomb of Hoehnê Wronski. He was a magician who preceded Aleister Crowley. Both were knowledgeable in a process known as spanning the "distance" although spatial distance is not involved. Amado explained to me that most people misconstrue spanning the distance to mean going from the physical plane to the astral plane. This is not correct. The world we live in is here and now, like Zen masters teach. This is our "reality" in which we exist. But the world "there" is a different reality into which we may wander on occasions. Spanning the distance means to go from "here" to "there". Between the two worlds is a transformational state.

This information from Amado is strikingly similar to what Mr. X told me about Aleister Crowley travelling from one world to the other. It has everything to do with the travelling to other time zones. All of this leads us straight to the enigma of the Wilson brothers.

CHAPTER THIRTY-THREE

33

THE WILSON
MOON CHILDREN

In the chapter on the Wilson clan it was mentioned that the twin brothers were sterile and that this would provide a clue for those who are familiar with magick. This has to do with the subject of virgin births.

To my surprise, I discovered during this investigation that virgin births are a medical fact and not just miraculous stories from the Bible. They are not common but are written up in medical journals from time to time. Many ordinary people are aware of this oddity but most are not. I have heard many debates over the divinity of Jesus during my life. If this one oddity were recognized, it would have changed the entire context of those debates. Actually, I hope that my bringing the subject to light in this book will change the entire context of how humanity looks at itself. The information which follows has been supplied by Madame X and is written with a bit of medicalese but is based upon esoteric doctrine (medical doctors are not trained or qualified to go beyond the physical plane). Those interested in the purely biological aspects should consult a state of the art medical library.

Sterility in twins is a sign of a virgin birth.

219

A virgin birth refers to interdimensional mating and results in what is called a Moonchild or Sexchild. This is also a sterile birth, and the sterility results from the interdimensional mating.

On a physical level, a virgin (or even any other woman) can be impregnated and not know how. This is the result of a latent male protein from the father that resides in all females but cannot be found unless it is triggered. It is in fact an acid that acts just like a sperm and penetrates the zona pellucida, a protective body which contains a sack. The zona pellucida is very hard to penetrate. If it wasn't, any old sperm or perhaps anything else (like animal sperm), could come in and be a candidate for gestation.

Normal pregnancy occurs when the native (or psychic) intelligence in the cell receives a message that a sperm is out there waiting to enter. If the proper biological conditions are present, the sperm is permitted access. In the case of a virgin birth, the protein is activated to act like a sperm and "fools" the zona pellucida into thinking it's a sperm. A child is eventually born with the gestation period usually lasting ten months.

The protein referred to above is located in the body's original cells which are eight in number and located at the base of the spine. This is the root of "kundalini" and is the first physical base of life where spirit first united with matter. These eight cells are juxtaposed in a geometrical fashion that consists of two pyramids. Four cells make up a pyramid or tetrahedron. The other four make another similar pyramid. The two tetrahedrons then interlock, upside down to each other. If you were to take a two dimensional side view, this cell structure would look like the Seal of Solomon, more popularly recognized as the Star of David.

This geometric structure contains all the wisdom of the universe and can be tapped either psychically or electromagnetically. (This is also the exact point where Montauk boys have had incisions for abduction purposes). This tetrahedral structure is what is penetrated by the magician when a Moonchild is created. His own consciousness or psychic/sexual energy (which is electromagnetic in nature) is taking the latent protein within the center of the tetrahedrons and is awakening the kundalini within the zona pellucida. A magical child is thus created.

The timing in this has to be very exact and there are countless other factors that we won't go into. What is important is that this method is used to create a Christ or Antichrist. It is also quite possible that a third party besides the magician could come into play. For example, the magician could be a vehicle for the Holy Spirit or for something sinister.

As has been suggested before, the major mystery schools of this planet make a profession out of these types of operations. The scope of this book will not begin to attempt to describe the various motivations and scenarios of such groups. It is enough to know that making Moonchildren is a serious subject that has vast repercussions. Balancing the Christ energy with the Antichrist energy has everything to do with the subject of time and how we became entrapped in this locale.

If the Wilson brothers were Moonchildren, it would seem to explain a lot. The key would have to do with their general genealogy and exactly who their parents were. That is currently being researched, but it is difficult to say the least. The genealogy shows that there is a link to the Cameron clan. In the grand design of creation, it would stand to reason that certain names or lineages would be chosen to fulfill certain roles or destinies.

Next, we should consider the Montauk legend of Duncan Cameron being reborn in 1951. According to that, Alexander Duncan Cameron Sr. got word from the future that he should have another baby. After first siring a daughter, his son Duncan rearrived on the scene. If Duncan was trained to be an Antichrist, it stands to reason that there was a magician behind his birth (this is not meant to imply that Duncan's birth was a virgin one, although that possibility cannot be entirely ruled out). Was it Duncan Sr. or was it Crowley? We don't know, only that there is considerable synchronicity between the two families.

In the case of the Wilson brothers, we have to wonder if their magician was any of the above. It could even have been Crowley or Duncan Sr. in an earlier life. All we can do is speculate at this point.

If we try and keep to the same logic as the above legend, we can postulate (and after all, that is what good magicians do best!) that Father Wilson or Mother Wilson was contacted in much the same way that Duncan Sr. was. The Wilson brothers were subsequently born and created an avenue through time whereby Crowley or whoever could work their magick through the space-time continuum. This entire family of Wilsons, Camerons, etc. would seem to be the agents of some force that has tremendous influence on the continuum. The goodness or badness of this force is not the pertinent point. We have to rise above duality if we want to understand the mechanism behind it all.

Going back to the Babalon Working, we have an event which transcends the boundaries of space and time. Cameron and Hubbard are both interesting family players in that they are Wilsons and apparently come from the same gene pool. Jack Parsons would seem to be somewhat of an outsider and ended up conflicting with Crowley. Did

Jack give us the Wilsons? Was it Crowley?

I ran my theory by Cameron, and she said there could be something to it. She agreed undoubtedly that there is a very mysterious connection. Perhaps she will reveal more as time goes by.

This entire subject has given us many ponderables and it is extremely likely that we will get some answers in the future. The objective here is to lay open the playing field and thereby open the door to further investigation. That inevitably leads to more truth.

EPILOGUE

The original purpose of this book was to corroborate that the Montauk Project took place in some form. If my experiences and the accounts of others are believed, it becomes obvious. Most people do not want to look at what makes themselves tick, let alone the universe. This fact alone has made the investigation difficult.

The occult factors and synchronicities I have relayed came totally as an unexpected surprise to me. It has been a long hard journey experiencing, collecting and writing all this information. Even though we are at the end of this leg of the journey, the horizon is filled with intriguing potentials and many new adventures await.

I find the Babalon Working to be one of the most fascinating synchronicities, not only because of what was being attempted but because of the characters involved. No major work has been attempted on this subject to date. Cameron has had countless interviews, but the writers always want to know about Jack. They abuse her by ignoring her. In fact, she was the result of the Babalon Working and her life has demonstrated that. Cameron holds the keys to many mysteries, the most important of which is the unleashing of womankind. This has already begun but has a long way yet to go. When I initially met Cameron, I discussed the possibility of writing such a

225

book. While this may still happen, there is no firm commitment from either party. She has also expressed interest in writing her own book about the Babalon Working.

In the same breath as Cameron, we must consider the stories of conspiracy that have surrounded the Jet Propulsion Laboratory. According to some accounts, Jack Parsons was practically worshipped by key members of that organization. In any event, he was definitely respected. Much of the light shown on him in this book was the result of a staff member of the Jet Propulsion Laboratory contacting me out of the blue and giving me some of the information I've included. He enthusiastically studies Parsons and will provide me with any further data that he finds. This story is apparently just opening up.

Also on the horizon is Amado Crowley. He may hold the trump card yet; only time will tell. On the 50th anniversary of his father's death, he intends to publish some explosive documents that will indicated his father was murdered and that his legal will was altered. As Crowley died on December 1, 1947, we will have to wait until 1997 to see if those documents will have any serious repurcussions. Madame X tells me that this information has already reverberated throughout the different mystery schools and is of the utmost concern. Amado has promised to give more information as the timing of circumstances allow.

Perhaps the biggest clue to the Crowley connection concerns the family's heraldic Coat-of-Arms. It equates to the tarot card "The Sun" in Crowley's Thoth Tarot Deck. This concerns the New Aeon (New Age in today's vernacular) and the emancipation of the human race. Maybe the incredible thread of synchronicities between the Crowleys, Camerons and Wilsons is just an old magical formula built within the structure of the universe that is telling us that it is time for Mankind to be free. It is safe to come out of the woodwork.

Whatever the case with Aleister Crowley, his knowledge is a tool. Like a hammer, it can be used for good or evil. It is up to each of us to determine the outcome.

And last, but not least, is the research of Preston, Duncan and Al Bielek. New information about Montauk, its ramifications and other projects continues to come in. There is no shortage of excitement or lack of avenues to pursue in our quest for understanding the universe(s).

We will talk to you again later.

L. RON HUBBARD

An incredible amount of nonsense has been written about this man. I will be brief as possible and stick to the salient points based upon my own personal knowledge and insights.

Hubbard was extremely wide read and had an acute aptitude for the paranormal. His experiences were not those of a "normal" person and he was continually finding that nobody believed him. Various authors and courts have condemned him for being a compulsive liar. I definitely found this not to be true in my own experience, but if he was a compulsive liar to some, it was partly because no one believed him when he told the truth. Why not just tell them something that works? Hubbard believed in workability beyond all else and he was extremely effective in his pursuits. He hated the establishment because it furthered stagnation and was a hallmark of ineffectiveness.

The Navy career of L. Ron Hubbard is checkered with ambiguity. His actual Naval records will not be released although there is agreement that he worked in Naval Intelligence. This being the case, disinformation as to his whereabouts and duties would have been fabricated as a matter of due course.

It is known that Hubbard studied the psychiatric records of Navy personnel and had information on the cutting edge procedures of the day. This included narcosynthesis and regression techniques. He took what he learned from psychiatric research, plus his earlier studies, and formulated Dianetics. This was the first major regression therapy applied on a broad basis and was designed to be easy for the layman to use.

Hubbard also studied Aleister Crowley and found him fascinating. Crowley's principles are to be found here and there throughout Hubbard's work, but they are not one and the same thing. Hubbard developed his own techniques and was more of an innovator than a copycat.

Hubbard's popularity grew and he never had to look back as far as money was concerned. The Church of Scientology grew out of this popularity and it was incorporated as a legal religion in 1954. Hubbard had constant difficulties running organizations and found he couldn't openly trust others to "just go do it". He formulated his own administrative system and set it up to be effective. The purpose was to sell books and get his Dianetics and Scientology processes to the public. He honestly believed this would save humanity.

The Government waged decades of war against Hubbard and much of it was unconstitutional. I believe that they were angry at him for breaking security with information he had obtained while with the Navy. His organization was also perceived as a threat by J. Edgar Hoover, Richard Nixon and other establishment forces.

I first saw Hubbard in 1972 and Scientology was a growing and dynamic movement at that point. He had definite health problems, but they were not exaggerated nor did they seem to hamper him. These were not hidden from the crew. He considered himself an experimental guinea pig and what he released as standard Scientology was watered down (as far as being dangerous) and foolproof as far as he was concerned.

Hubbard is often described as a temperamental hot head who always had to get his way. He had extremely high expectations and they were not often met. Very often, he didn't get his way and nothing was done about it for a long time or sometimes not at all. Of course, there were plenty of times when he achieved what he wanted, but he was mostly busy researching. Hubbard did not constantly police anyone. At times, he would keep to himself but he never ignored the crew. I only saw him get angry a couple of times and this was after a person had repeatedly acted like a fool.

Hubbard said he had no idea he would become so popular and become such a figurehead. Had he known, he would have led his life much differently. It was wild and filled with outrageous aspects. In fact, he told a friend of mine in the early 1970's that he would prefer to die. His body was worn out, and he felt he had to keep it alive because he had become an important symbol to so many people that followed the movement.

Government agents reportedly used to take bets on how fast they could put Hubbard in prison. Although they were not successful in this regard, I believe he was under constant psychotronic attack during the time the Montauk Project was in operation. He even ended up on Long Island during most of 1973.

The Church of Scientology grew to be a very large organization by the early 1980's. Despite high officials going to prison for conspiracy against the Government, the movement was highly popular and growing. In 1981, at what was probably the height of the Church's popularity, Hubbard was no longer directly involved. He was hiding so as not to be served with a subpoena. Several people thought the movement had been infiltrated by the CIA pitting one Scientology faction against another. There was tremendous infighting within the organization during this period and the majority of people I knew left. The organization totally changed its operating basis and hasn't been the same since.

Hubbard passed on in January 1986 at the age of 74. He called his confidante, Pat Broeker, to his room a few days before he departed and told him that he would be leaving his body. Hubbard was concerned that people might grieve and cry over his departure. He said this wasn't necessary and that people would cry only because of their own self-invalidation. In other words, people would be crying over their own belief system that they themselves were not immortal.

I've tried to be as objective as possible about this short biographical sketch of Hubbard. It is important to realize that this man had incredible knowledge. He wanted the entire world to access it. If he were clearly interested in money and power and that was all, he would have led a much more extravagant life style. Most of the time, his quarters were not as plush as the average three bedroom house. His life was also filled with pits and valleys and he would have been the first to agree. The man has simply not been accurately portrayed in any biographical accounts of him.

I believe that the real clues to this man's role on Earth have to do with his involvement with Jack Parsons and his heritage with the Wilson clan. His activities there are still shrouded in mystery.

B

ALEISTER CROWLEY

Aleister Crowley was born in 1875 and given the name Edward Alexander which he used until his late teens. His father, also named Edward Alexander Crowley, was a wealthy brewer who became a fire and brimstone preacher.

Crowley's brilliance as a young child is legendary. He reportedly learned the game of chess after watching one match and was virtually unbeatable thereafter. He led a privileged life except for the fact that he was force fed the Christian religion in a most abhorrent manner. Perhaps the best illustration of this is an incident that took place as a young teen at the private school he attended.

The teacher had caught wind of an outbreak of homosexuality among Crowley's classmates. One of the perpetrators was caught and was forced under the whip to tell on his accomplices. Crowley was named as being a guilty party although he would deny his involvement for his entire life. (This is particularly noteworthy as Crowley never denied being involved in homosexuality in later life.) The teacher then proceeded to extract a confession from Crowley and flogged him repeatedly. He was forced to recite Christian prayers between floggings under the assumption that he would see the errors of his ways. Unfortunately, Crowley didn't know what he was accused of, but he was beaten repeatedly for a period of about two weeks. The teacher finally became exasperated and told Crowley what he suspected. Crowley told him he would have confessed to that right away if he'd only known what he wanted to hear. The teacher became disgusted and expelled Crowley.

Upon returning home to his mother with the expulsion notice, she read the scandal and said words that are now famous. They were something like the following.

"You're a beast. Yes. You're the beast of revelation — 666!"

Young Crowley felt very relieved to hear these words because he could identify with them. Anything that was anti-Christian must be good because Christianity had proven itself to be the most evil thing in the world in his own mind.

The above experience is usually overlooked when books are written about Crowley. It is perhaps one of the most revelatory experiences in his early life.

Crowley's father died when he was twelve. He lived under the care of his mother and an uncle until he went to Cambridge University. There, he studied the physcial sciences and had a renaissance education. He is arguably one of the more skilled poets ever. In any case, he had a mastery of the English language (and many others too).

At the age of twenty he inherited a fortune and abandoned the last year of his formal education. He was now enthusiastically pursuing the occult and studied in many secret societies. He would later rise to the highest leadership position in many ancient orders. The Masons, Rosicrucians, Order of the Silver Star and Ordo Templi Orientis are amongst them. The latter, commonly referred to as the O.T.O. is perhaps the most significant in his own life. While being the Outer Head of the O.T.O., he formulated and wrote down his most famous work, *Magick, in Theory and Practice*. He spelled "magick" with a "k" so as to differentiate it from parlor magic.

The most spectacular event in Crowley's life occurred in 1904 at the Boulak Museum in Cairo. Crowley and his wife Rose had recently spent the night in the King's Chamber of the Great Pyramid. While staying at a flat in Cairo, Rose fell into a foreign state of mind and kept repeating that Crowley had offended Horus, the Egyptian god. Crowley was mystified as his wife knew virtually nothing about Egyptian mythology. She then proceeded to tell him how to invoke Horus and finally dragged him to the Boulak Museum. There, he was shocked. Rose showed him an image of Horus in a form known as Ra-Hoor-Khuit. The display number was "666". This experience resulted in a tremendous illumination which would change the course of Crowley's life forever.

Soon after, at midnight on March 19th, he declared that the equinox of the gods had arrived and that a new epoch in human history had begun. Crowley subsequently dictated a message from Aiwas, his own Holy Guardian Angel, which would serve as a link between the solar spiritual forces and mankind.

This message was written down in what became known as "The Book of the Law". This work lays down a simple code of conduct which is "Do what thou wilt shall be the whole of the law. Love is the law, love under will. There is no law beyond Do what thou wilt."

These words are often misinterpreted, particularly when they are spoken of on TV talk shows and written about by authors who are not serious students. Such persons might say that the above doctrine encourages others to do what they want, such as murder, rape, and pillage. This is very far from the true teaching.

Crowley taught that every man and woman was a star. Each of us is to move on our true orbit, marked by the nature of our position, the law of our growth and the impulse of our past experiences.

According to this same doctrine, all events are equally lawful and everyone is necessary in theory. In practice, only one act is lawful for each of us at any given moment. Therefore, it is our duty to determine to experience the right event from one moment of consciousness to another.

It should also be noted that "thelema", the Greek word for "will", has the same numerical value as "agape", the Greek word for "love". This is not considered to be an accident. Each action or motion is an act of love that will unite with the whole. Each act must be "under will", chosen so as to fulfill and not thwart the true nature of the being concerned.

The technical methods of achieving this are to be studied in Crowley's system of "Magick".

It is important to know that Crowley's life was full of scandal. Much of it had to do with sex, drugs and strange rites. Sometimes he was accussed of murder such as sacrificing his son MacAleister. When you realize that he had no son by the name of MacAleister, you begin to understand that what has been said about this man is not usually accurate. He did have quite a reputation as a sorcerer or magician and some people were quite afraid of him. He was never jailed and some say that is simply because he was such a good magician.

Crowley was definitely a trickster and there are those who believe that he created a cloud around his activities so as to repel those who were not worthy of the knowledge he had to teach. A case can be made for this as he once hired a secretary, whom he referred to as the Ape of Thoth, to write scandal and circulate rumors about him.

I should also warn the reader that the average person who reads Crowley's works may find himself repelled mentally, morally or both. If this occurs, understand that repulsion is a reverse magnetism and is forcing one not to look at something. One often has to get past that to discover the truth. But if the repulsion is too strong, it may be best to stay away from the material. It is far easier to whimper off to the refrigerator and munch on a fudgesicle.

It is quite possible to be appalled by the grossness of the internal combustion engine. Without a muffler, it is absolutely horrendous and quite repulsive indeed. But if the sound is muffled and the engine works, no one thinks twice about driving the car to get to where he is going.

Whatever the case, Crowley dedicated his life trying to give others the keys to drive out of this universe. He coined the phrase "THE WAY OUT IS THROUGH".

There is much controversy surrounding the life of Aleister Crowley. The principles he illustrated are far more important than the person himself. I think if he were here today, he would tell us one thing:

GET OUT!

C

THE SHELLEYS

When my psychic friend Joy told me she had been channeling the name Duncan Cameron for over a year and a half, I asked her for further information. The name "Wilson" came with it, along with a name like "Shelby", which I later identified as "Shelley". This name, of course, refers to Percy and Mary Shelley. Percy was a master of the English language and considered by some to be the best writer ever. Mary authored the book *Frankenstein*. They lived an exotic and creative life on the edge of society. Their exploits have been romanticized for years, both on stage and in countless books.

Joy had told me that the Wilson Brothers had a connection to Geneva. This city is very close to where the Shelley's were living when they told the midnight stories that eventually resulted in *Frankenstein*. Geneva has long been considered in legend to be the world headquarters of the Illuminati or some such conspiratorial organization.

I checked several books but came up with no significant connections between the Shelleys and any Camerons or Wilsons. I did however check with Marjorie Cameron and she told me an interesting story about Dennis Murphy. He authored the book *The Sergeant* and inspired a character in *East of Eden* by John Steinbeck. Murphy's family settled in the beautiful redwood studded area of Big Sur in Northern California, near Santa Cruz. The family eventually founded the Esalen Institute, an avant-garde training school that deals with metaphysical topics and is always considered "very California" and on the "cutting edge". Cameron thought a great deal of Dennis Murphy.

When I told Cameron about the Shelleys possibly being connected to the Wilsons, I asked her if she had any information on a possible connection. She told me that one time Murphy had taken her to a very special spot in Big Sur. There seemed to be no other agenda than his taking her to some cliffs and pointing to the ivy that was growing there. He told her that the ivy had initially been transplanted from Percy Shelley's grave. It was odd. Why had he gone out of his way to show this to her? Cameron didn't have any more information for me other than that.

I then called my friend Kenn Arthur and asked him if he knew anything about the Shelleys. He said that Percy Shelley and Lord Byron (for those who don't know already, he was the most famous writer of his day and was a trio with the Shelleys in Geneva) were bisexual. He joked that Mary Shelley was trisexual. In other words, she'd "try" anything. This being true, it is not a far leap to guess that they might have been involved in sexual magick in their own right. The concept of Dr. Frankenstein's monster certainly identifies with a magical child albeit an aborted one.

Kenn said that there was a mystic named Marcia Moore who had done past life regressions with her group. Three of the people had turned up past lives being Percy, Mary and Lord Byron. He referred me to a book but it could not be found. When I told him about the ivy from Shelley's grave at Big Sur, Kenn said that explained it.

Marcia Moore disappeared from the face of the Earth at Big Sur in the 1970's. It was one of the major metaphysical mysteries of the century.

I looked into Marcia Moore and found out that she was a very beautiful woman who was a yoga teacher. She lived in Manhattan and Massachusetts before going to California. She had children and apparently took excellent care of them. She was not a "kook" in any sense of the word.

Marcia was experimenting with certain herbs and was actually trying to transcend the physical plane by invoking higher consciousness. Her disappearance was a total mystery as far as the police were concerned. I took her picture to psychic Maria Fix and had her read on it. She'd never heard of Marcia Moore but immediately said that the woman was beyond this dimension. I told her the circumstances surrounding her disappearance, and Maria read that two gentlemen had found her in the woods and murdered her. The body was well hidden and never recovered. She also said that the murderers were friends from a previous life and were giving Marcia what she wanted: transcendence. Marcia was shocked and extremely disoriented after the death. She eventually regained her bearings and had achieved what she wanted. Just like the sailors on the *U.S.S. Eldridge*, Marcia was jolted out of this dimension. If Maria's psychic reading is correct, Marcia Moore's spiritual training put her in better stead than the average crew member of the *Eldridge*.

Further investigation would show that Big Sur sits on the same parallel as Norfolk, Virginia. There is also a psychiatric hospital in the area with a huge underground facility. Both Al Bielek and one of the Norfolk triplets (see Chapter 24) has informed me that there was a version of the Montauk Project at Big Sur.

There is also another interesting aspect to the Shelley investigation. There was an actual Castle Frankenstein and it can still be visited today. In my search, I ran across a book entitled *In Search of Frankenstein* by Radu Florescu. He researched Mary Shelley's notes from the time period and shows that they likely visited the castle. The Shelleys apparently stopped at a wayside inn and got drunk listening to tales and legends. Some of the peasants believed these two strangers were in some way related to the Frankenstein clan.

Florescu extensively researched the Frankenstein clan and gives considerably more information than I can relay here. One noteworthy ancestor was Baron Frank von Frankenstein who wrote a history on the origins of Transylvanian Germans. The Baron was adamant about refuting the legend of the "Pied Piper of Hamelin". According to that story, the children were led by the Pied Piper through a hole in a mountain and emerged in Transylvania to become the ancestors of the Germans in that area. Whether its true or not, this legend has a gripping similarity to the Aryan Montauk boys that were grasped at Montauk.

Of even more interest in this book is a young alchemist by the name of Johann Konrad Dippel. He was born in 1673 at Castle Frankenstein and signed his doctoral dissertation "Franckensteina" which was about "the principle of life". Because of his unorthodox views, he was expelled from the University of Strasbourg (Strasbourg was a city the Shelleys visited and was also where the Nazi gold treasure disappeared at the end of WW II).

The career of Dippel paralleled that of Mary Shelley's character Victor Frankenstein. He was quite brilliant and far ahead of his professors. Travelling to Sweden, he taught wherever he could but eventually made his way back to the University of Strasbourg. After a two year residence, he fled unexpectedly. There had been body snatching in a local cemetery and the locals gossiped that he had been involved. These sorts of rumors plagued him throughout his life.

Dippel returned to the study of alchemy and ended up back in Frankenstein country. The area was loaded with different alchemical laboratories and the castle itself housed one. He experimented with human body parts and animals and invented actual medicines and the artist's paint known as Prussian blue. Dippel's philosophy indicates a belief in magical ritual to give life. He became the victim of intrigues and continued to run from place to place. Dippel's life ended in an unnatural death and his own body disappeared.

A larger than life legend ensued after Dippel's death. Bands of alchemists and treasure seekers sought out his old haunts near the castle. While popular recorded history apparently has them all being unsuccessful in seeking treasure, this is not necessarily the case. If someone had actually found any spoils, they would have wisely perpetrated the story that nothing had been found. History would be none the wiser.

In Search of Frankenstein begins to give some real clues as to a thrilling history that is far stranger than ordinary legend. Unfortunately, scholarship and recorded history (which is often altered by the powers that be) can only reach so far. The author leaves us at the threshold of fascination when he talks about the exquisite clock makers of Switzerland of the 17th Century. The technology of the time period was so precise that robots were built that probably far exceeded at least the technology of the 1960's These robots could play a variety of songs with musical instruments but most were lost or taken away during the centuries. Occasionally, one can find a remnant in a European museum.

All of this gives rise to serious questions. What was going on in Geneva during the last few centuries? What was the power and technology behind the clock makers, also the seat of world finance? And, what was the symbology of creatures popping out of clocks?

Could all this mean to suggest that those who control the finances of the world also control and manipulate the consciousness of time?

May the intrigue continue.

D

CAMERON

Cameron is a poet and artist and is probably the most significant figure in the Goddess movement. Born in Belle Plain, Iowa*, a spiritual passion overtook her as a child and she became a center point for various forms of knowledge.

Cameron joined the U.S. Navy as Marjorie Cameron but began using her last name only after being called that during her entire military career. Working directly for the Joint Chiefs of Staff during WW II, she made maps and was the only enlisted person working for them at the time. She had occasion to witness unbelievable corruption and went A.W.O.L. when her brother was brought home in a straitjacket. Fearing that she might expose her own commanding officer, she was court martialed but it didn't appear in her records.

After serving in the Navy, she came into contact with Jack Parsons, the notable rocket scientist who co-founded Aerojet General Corporation. In a reversal of fortunes for the Navy, she married Jack and engaged in the now

---

* Belle Plain is the home of the largest artesian water well in the world. She believes this is significant because there is legend that this water well is connected through the underground to Loch Ness, where Aleister Crowley lived and gave rise to the legends of the Loch Ness Monster.

famous "Babalon Working". This was an ambitious sex magick ritual, the repercussions of which can still be felt today. Shortly after this operation, mass sightings of UFOs began to occur across the United States.

Cameron left her husband about a year later and sought out Aleister Crowley himself, thinking that she was his magical daughter. By the time she reached Paris, Crowley died. After this shocking news, she decided to enter a convent near Geneva, Switzerland. Three weeks later, she had one of the most profound experiences of her life. She found herself looking in front of a mirror and had a spontaneous reaction. She took off all her clothes and howled like a beast. This act removed any denial of her true human nature, and she returned to her husband in Pasadena.

When Jack Parsons died in 1952, Cameron moved to Mexico and associated with famous artists and writers there. A renegade Catholic priest tried to burn her at the stake during this period but his plans came to naught (he was also expelled from the Roman Catholic Church). She eventually returned to Los Angeles and continued to work as an actress, artist and poet. Her life continued to read like an adventure book and she married Sheridan Kimmel. He was the inspiration for Ken Kesey's character "McMurphy" in the book *One Flew Over the Cuckoos Nest.*

Cameron is not well known to the general public, but she has been one of the foremost revolutionaries of our time. She appeared in different underground movies and one of her visionary drawings resulted in the closing by the vice squad of a gallery exhibition. This broke new ground in setting artistic and legal precedent for freedom of expression. Her audio lecture series *Superwoman* is played regularly on Los Angeles radio and the world has yet to discover the depths and influence of this woman.

E

JACK PARSONS

In this book, we have already discussed the basic facts surrounding Jack Parsons and his unique life. There is considerable intrigue about this man which is apparently beyond the scope of this book but should be commented upon nevertheless.

As his contract work with rocketry resulted in the founding of Aerojet General Corporation and substantial government contracts (this all began prior to World War II), he was of keen interest to the military industrial complex. They also would have been very keen on his brilliance and technological capabilities. The fact that he was a magician would have either intrigued or irritated the military to no end. He was highly sought after and the Government watched him like a hawk.

One of the Government agents who spied on Parsons was supposedly L. Ron Hubbard. He claimed that he was sent in by Navy intelligence to bust up the practice of black magic amongst the scientists at Cal Tech. Cameron says the same might apply to herself, but whatever the case, they both got involved very deeply themselves. Hubbard would later credit Aleister Crowley in his Philadelphia Doctorate Course lectures so it is likely that he was involved on a personal and magical level.

The Magicians Dictionary quotes Colin Wilson as sayings that Parsons had been advised by a higher power "to declare war on all authority that is not based on courage and manhood...the authority of lying priests, conniving judges, blackmailing police and to call an end to restriction and inhibition, conscription, compulsion, regimentation and the tyranny of laws." The higher power was identified as Hubbard, but this did not come out until the late 1980's, after his death. This identification appears to have validity because it was revealed in several places at once.

Whatever Hubbard's actual role was, he did share secrets with Jack Parsons. Hubbard touted a book called *Excalibur* which supposedly described the secrets of life itself. According to legend, the people who read the manuscript went insane and he withdrew it. Parson's most significant work has been closely guarded as well. Both of these men were participants in what has been described as the most celebrated and significant sexual magick act of the 20th century. Cameron said both men never recovered.

Another one of Parsons best friends was Robert A. Heinlein, the "Dean of Science Fiction". Heinlein frequented the same haunts as Hubbard and both were made privy to the inner workings of magick and the O.T.O. Not insignificantly, they both were U.S. Naval officers. Heinlein made a big step toward changing the world when he wrote the book *Stranger in a Strange Land* which was a rallying point for what later became known as the hippie movement. He originated the word "grok" (meaning deep understanding) and based his entire work on the philosophy of the O.T.O. The relationship between Heinlein and Jack Parsons is covered brilliantly and in great detail in *Green Egg* magazine (Summer, Autumn and Winter editions of 1992).

Parsons knew many famous people but perhaps the most politically powerful was Howard Hughes, the czar of the fledgling aerospace industry. Cameron's research indicates that Hughes controlled the CIA after 1949. This time period is interesting because it occurs just after his famous plane crash. Hughes was an enthusiastic pilot and held world records. In the late 1940's, he was almost killed and went into a serious coma. The doctors thought he was dead or at least a vegetable case. He made a miraculous recovery, but it turned out not to be so miraculous. It was at this point that he became incredibly eccentric and just plain weird. It is speculative, but it is not a far stretch to guess that Hughes may have been resurrected by aliens who programmed him to do their bidding. The man had tremendous influence and this may have led to Parsons death.

If Hughes was a CIA monster, Jack Parsons' disdain for authority couldn't have helped him any. In June 1952, just before Cameron and he were to make a scheduled trip to Mexico, Parsons died in a laboratory experiment of mysterious origin. Popular and irresponsible accounts like to depict him as a suicide over his misfortunes with Hubbard or some other imagined enemy, but this is not the case. In fact, two explosions occurred that day and one was from under the floor boards. He didn't blow himself up. Somebody killed him, and Cameron is sure that Hughes was behind it. A very appropriate question to ask in this matter is "Who was behind Howard Hughes?"

Hubbard would state after Parsons' death that he was very fortunate to have known such a remarkable man as Jack Parsons. Two weeks after Jack died, the Capitol was stormed with UFOs. Serious Government pursuit of Hubbard began in earnest shortly thereafter. The world hasn't been quite the same since.

The Montauk Pulse™

A CHRONICLE OF TIME

As *The Montauk Project* originally went to press, many new and startling developments began to take place.

The Montauk Pulse began in January of 1993 in order to keep people up to date. We guaranteed at least two issues annually but are issuing one newsletter each quarter as the enthusiasm and information flow warrant it.

The Montauk Pulse contains six pages per issue and covers new breakthroughs and information on the Montauk story. Mr. Nichols is also continuing his research into time functions and any new developments regarding that will be reported as well as information on aliens that is deemed relevant to the human condition.

If you liked this book, you will enjoy the newsletter even more. No punches will be pulled!

Turn the page for ordering information.

Do You Know Someone Who Would Like The _Original_ Book That Started It All?

TITLE	QTY.	TOTAL
The Montauk Project: Experiments In Time..................$15.95		
Montauk Revisited: Adventures In Synchronicity........$19.95		
The Philadelphia Experiment & Other UFO Conspiracies....................................$12.95		
Fantastic Inventions of Nichola Tesla...........................$16.95		
Anti-Gravity & The World Grid....................................$14.95		
Anti-Gravity & The Unified Field................................$14.95		
The Anti-Gravity Handbook...$14.95		
The Montauk Tour Video...$39.95		
Montauk Project T-Shirt...$12.95		

SHIPPING RATES

UNDER $30.00 ....ADD $3.00
$30.01- 60.00 ....ADD $4.00
OVER 60.00...............ADD $6.00

FOREIGN COUNTRIES ADD $5.00
EXTRA FOR SURFACE SHIPPING

IN A HURRY? FOR 2 DAY
PRIORITY MAIL ADD $3.00

SUBTOTAL	
FOR DELIVERY IN NY ADD 8.5% TAX	
SHIPPING: SEE CHART TO THE LEFT	
PRIORITY MAIL	
TOTAL AMOUNT	

FOREIGN ORDERS MUST BE ACCOMPANIED BY A POSTAL MONEY ORDER IN U.S. FUNDS. ALL CHECKS MUST BE DRAWN ON A U.S. BANK. ALLOW 30 DAYS FOR U.S. DELIVERY.

SEND CHECK PAYABLE TO: SKY BOOKS, BOX 769, WESTBURY, NEW YORK 11590.

SOLD TO:

SHIP TO: (only if different than sold to)

QUANTITY ORDERS
If you would like to order in quantity, please write to the Sales Dept. at the above address.

"What a long strange trip it's been."

*Robert Hunter,
lyricist for the Grateful Dead*